DANIEL BĂNULESCU

WHO WON THE WORLD WAR OF RELIGIONS?

Translated by Alistair Ian Blyth

Featured Artist
Isur Isar

University of Plymouth Press

20 ROMANIAN WRITERS SERIES

Daniel Bănulescu's *Who Won the World War of Religions?* is the eighth title to be published in the series 20 Romanian Writers by the University of Plymouth Press. The series is one aspect of the University of Plymouth's ongoing commitment to introduce Romania's vibrant artistic culture to other nations. In addition to the literature, the University of Plymouth will be hosting a series of exhibitions and performances of Romania's visual and musical arts over the next five years. The following supplement features one of Romania's leading contemporary artists.

Featured Artist

ISUR ISAR

Isur Isar (born 1961) is a graduate of the Tonitza School of Fine Art, Bucharest and an active member of Romania's Visual Artists' Union. He is widely regarded as one of Romania's most exceptional art teachers, respected for his dedication in promoting and nurturing young artistic talent. Isar's work is driven by a desire to communicate with those around him, as well as his inner self, through connecting with the 'vibrations of the soul that generate artistic attitudes'. He enjoys mixing and experimenting with a diverse range of materials in his quest to enhance the expressivity of his message, consciously resisting stepping into the trap of routine and repetition. His compositions convey a dream or story through the interfusion of the chimerical and the absolute. The resultant effects are elusive and fragmentary. Like Bănulescu's play, Isar's work offers a form of surreal commentary upon the Romanian psyche and contemporary states of being.

Winner of the 2002 Prize for Etching at the Romanian Annual Engraving Contest, Isar has exhibited both at home and abroad; locations include Paris, Venice and Sao Paolo. Over the past decade he has coordinated creative camps in Romania, such as the Youth Etching Camp (2008) and the Icon Glass-Painting Camp (2007, 2008).

Liz Wells

DANIEL BĂNULESCU

WHO WON THE WORLD WAR OF RELIGIONS?

Translated by Alistair Ian Blyth

Contents

Alistair Ian Blyth

Saving Romanian Literature: Introducing Daniel Bănulescu

Recent Romanian literature has been dominated by two distinct 'movements', in the broadest sense of the term, each corresponding to two distinct periods: 'optzecism' (eighties-ism) and 'nouazecism' (nineties-ism). Whereas it is often quite hard to pinpoint any definite cut-off point between decades when taken as socio-cultural periods in which a particular mood or style is prevalent (the sixties, for example, cannot necessarily be said to have ended abruptly in December 1969), in the case of *optzecism* and *nouazecism* the date of the cleavage can be precisely fixed as having occurred in late December 1989. Broadly speaking, *eighties-ism* includes all the disparate forms of postmodernism that existed in Romanian literature under the conditions of a totalitarian state, while *nineties-ism* is that same literary postmodernism now liberated from official censorship, but under the conditions of a turbulent, chaotic post-communist social, economic and political transition period.

Daniel Bănulescu can be said to have made two debuts as a writer, firstly as an 'eighties-ist' and subsequently as a 'nineties-ist'. After his first, youthful poems appeared in *Amfiteatru* magazine in 1981, Bănulescu went on to publish, in 1987, a thirty-two page booklet containing twenty poems, entitled, at the last minute, *The Day on which I was Published*, the seventh in a series of supplements included in *Convingeri Comuniste* magazine (*Communist Convictions*—humourously, but unofficially known as *Coco*, for short). The booklet had already been typeset and was about to go to press when the censors summoned the author to the printers in the dead of night and obligated him to change the original title, which was *With Love and with Determination, Champagne*. Likewise, the censors struck fifteen of the initial poems from the collection. The published booklet also contained two brief presentations by critics Mircea Martin, who in the 1980s organised the regular Universitas literary cenacle in which Daniel Bănulescu also took part, and Laurențiu Ulici, at that time president of the Writers' Union of Romania. Mircea Martin observes that Bănulescu is "visibly incommoded and indisposed by conventional postures and big words," he is "preoccupied, even obsessed with aspects of the Eros," but has a "horror of sentimentalism." Ulici discovers in Bănulescu's poems a shift away from the metaphorical mode then prevalent in Romanian poetry, and towards the quasi-allegorical, towards a direct encounter with the real world, however painful or disappointing. Unlike in the work of other contemporary poets, this engagement with the real world is not aimed at discovering the poetry latent in the quotidian, but rather at expressing the poet's own attitude towards it.

Both Mircea Martin and Laurenţiu Ulici detected traces of "lexical violence" in Bănulescu's 'eighties-ist' debut, a violence that was to be given free rein in the poet's explosive 'nineties-ist' debut in 1993, a collection entitled *I'll Love you to the End of the Bed*. The volume was prefaced with a short autobiographical statement by the poet, which concludes, in the third person: "Although he knows hundreds of his peers more talented than him, with humility and sparing words the author glimpses but three great chances for Romanian literature: Daniel Bănulescu the poet, Daniel Bănulescu the novelist and Daniel Bănulescu the playwright." This was accompanied by a highly ramified genealogical table in which the lineage of Daniel Bănulescu and "the rest of the Bănulescu family" is traced back through, among many others, *The Master and Margarita*, J. D. Salinger, The Beatles, George Bacovia, the Prophet Daniel, Mihai Eminescu, Dalí, Dire Straits, and finally John the Baptist and Magheru Boulevard (the main artery of central Bucharest), each begotten by the Bible.

The volume caused a great stir in the literary press, being described variously as "iconoclastic, absurd, anarchic, swaggering, aggressive," and as "convincingly, therefore ironically, mimicking abysmal psychologism, but also attitudes bordering on juvenile delinquency." Laurenţiu Ulici now pointed to the "non-conformism, eroticism verging on the pornographic, taunted taboos, delusions of grandeur, caustic soda (or rather vitriol) poured over cosy hypocritical pudor, sexual delirium, vehement, allegro rhetoric, irony and self-irony, garrulousness, madness and despair" in Bănulescu's poetry, describing him as a "nineties-ist Villon," a comparison that was also to be made by a number of other critics. Writing a number of years after the book's initial, explosive impact, Nicolae Ţone imagines *I'll Love you to the End of the Bed* as having been "a huge revolver, with a red-hot barrel, aimed with nonchalance by the author primarily at the forehead of the literary world, and concomitantly at the foreheads of his contemporaries." Such a poetic attitude or persona could only arise and flourish in the 'nineties-ist' context, of course. It would have been impossible, for reasons external to literature, in the 'eighties-ist' period, although at that time it was recognised by critics Mircea Martin and Laurenţiu Ulici as latent in Bănulescu's work, as we have seen. From the wider perspective of twentieth-century Romanian literary history, however, Bănulescu's ironically swaggering attitude and glee in thumbing his nose at his "contemporaries" finds its counterpart and precedent in the pre-communist regime avant-garde of the inter-war years, exemplified, as Nicolae Țone points out, by works such as Geo Bogza's *Sex Diary* and *Invective Poem* and by the "terribiliste" writers of the 1930s—Gherasim Luca, Sesto Pals, Aurel Baranga, Paul Păun, Perahim et al.—who used to boast that they had "petrol in their testicles."

Whereas Daniel Bănulescu appears on the back cover of *I'll Love You to the End of the Bed* in a photographic collage of himself with a miniature ballerina twirling on his shoulder, on the front cover of his second collection of poems, *The Ballad of Daniel Bănulescu*, published in 1997, he is pictured with the back of his head turned toward the viewer, a pose which, of course, did not go unobserved by the critics and was interpreted in various ways—as defiance, for example, or as the poet gazing into his own text. It should also be noted that the book was part of a series—*Poets of the City of Bucharest*—each with the same format of cover design and a photograph of the respective poet, thus making Bănulescu's gesture of turning his back all the more provocative. Also generally noted was the fact that the author's name did not appear separately on the cover, but only as part of the title, which, on title page, included the following parenthesis: *The Ballad of Daniel Bănulescu (picked and fashioned by himself)*. Framed by a Prologue and Epilogue, the collection is a cycle of seventeen autobiographical poems, written in various linguistic registers and poetic forms (free verse, traditional rhyming quatrains, the prose poem, and even a collage of seemingly ready-made texts, in this case paediatrician's notes), each connected to a specific place in Bucharest. *I'll Love You to the End of the Bed* and *The Ballad of Daniel Bănulescu* were subsequently republished as a single volume in 2000 by Editura Vinea, with the title *The Federal Republic of Daniel Bănulescu: Northern State and Southern State*, another example of Bănulescu's ludic inflation of the authorial persona.

In accordance with his ironically self-aggrandising redemptive plan for Romanian literature, as stated in the Preface to his first (nineties-ist) collection of poems—"Daniel Bănulescu the poet, Daniel Bănulescu the novelist, and Daniel Bănulescu the playwright"—Bănulescu's second published work, in the year after *I'll Love you to the End of the Bed*, was a novel, with the equally provocative title *I Kiss Your Arse, Beloved Leader!* (1994). Once again, Bănulescu deliberately sets out to break all the rules, writing a book that is radically new and against the grain even in the context of 'nineties-ist' Romanian literature. At a time when Romanian letters more broadly, following the overthrow of the communist regime and the demise of state censorship, were dominated by testimonies and memoirs of life under totalitarianism, *I Kiss Your Arse Beloved Leader!* was a magical realist novel in which one of the main characters was none other than Ceauşescu himself, but a Ceauşescu who is cultivated, urbane, a gifted organist, and a visionary, who from superior cunning merely simulates the philistinism, semi-literacy, paranoia and mental obtuseness of the real Ceauşescu. In contrast to the narratives of political dissidence and "resistance through culture" prevalent at the time, in the novel Ceauşescu and the Securitate are pitted against the criminal underworld—the only genuine threat to their supremacy—and youthful master thief Swallow-Wort (in Romanian folklore, this is a herb with magical properties, including that of being able to open any lock). In this and other novels, Daniel Bănulescu displays an encyclopaedic knowledge of underworld, prison and gypsy slang, which forms a counterpoint to the rival literary discourses of the 'eighties-ists' and 'nighties-ists' (at the end of the book, Bănulescu even ludically "curses" a dozen literary rivals).

The ludic fictionalisation of the past is mirrored in Bănulescu's literary-historical fictionalisation of himself, in an absurd key: the back-cover blurb of the book contains quotations purporting to be from Gheorghe Panu, a nineteenth-century literary critic ("Immortal shall remain the mornings when I used to glimpse Mihai Eminescu and Daniel Bănulescu pedalling down the avenue, young and happy, accosting and racing lady passers-by, deriding the Muses, not at all mindful of their destiny as national writers," *Souvenirs de la jeunesse*); critic, Communist Party apparatchik and, post-1989, senator for the Greater Romania Party Mihai Ungheanu ("This piece of shit finished evening school at the same time as he finished off his mental health," press conference); and inter-war literary critic Mihalache Dragomirescu ("It is our belief that Romanian literature will once and for all be divided into literature before Daniel Bănulescu and literature after Daniel Bănulescu," *The Theory of the Masterpiece*), among others.

The book itself was caught up in a farcical series of occurrences when an event to launch it, in the spa town of Băile Herculane, in October 1994, was arbitrarily banned by the local mayor. The event happened to coincide with the arrival of President Ion Iliescu to speak at a Congress on Romanian Spirituality and to launch his own book, *Revolution and*

Reform. The local authorities and congress organisers were deaf to the fact that the "Beloved Leader" in the title of Bănulescu's novel referred not to Iliescu but to Ceauşescu and that the timing of the two launches was a pure coincidence. The owner of the bookshop where the launch of *I Kiss Your Arse, Beloved Leader!* was due to be held was given "friendly advice" not even to display the offending book, lest "the boys" pay him a visit and his windows get broken. The demonised, bewildering, Bulgakovian infra-reality of communist Romania described in the novel could certainly be said to have its counterpoint in the "diavoliad" of the murky, chaotic years of the post-Revolution transition. For, beyond the characters, the main "protagonist" of the novel, as Horia Gârbea argues, is ultimately the all-pervading unreality that held sway under the Ceauşescu regime, enveloping victims and executioners alike.

Daniel Bănulescu's second novel, *The Seven Kings of the City of Bucharest* (1998), is a fantastical tale set during the communist period, over seven days in 1988, in which the devil comes to Bucharest, arriving at Otopeni Airport, and recruits seven disciples, the "seven kings" of the title, who each perform seven miracles. The same as in *I Kiss Your Arse, Beloved Leader!*, the novel's cast features a host of fantastical characters, but also real persons, including Ceauşescu, critic Mircea Martin and other literary figures, and Daniel Bănulescu himself. In 2009, Daniel Bănulescu symbolically killed off his first novel, *I Kiss Your Arse, Beloved Leader!*, republishing it in extensively rewritten form as *Flee from Your Revolting and Hideous Life into My Book.* In the Preface to the resurrected and transformed novel, he describes how he "dynamited the casemate" of the old novel, salvaging nothing but a window frame and a chimney for the new book. Henceforth, *I Kiss Your Arse, Beloved Leader!* is banned from further publication and even mention (another example of Bănulescu exerting ludic "totalitarian" control over his work, complementing the ironic "cult of personality" he has established as author/ruler of his own "federal republic"). The new novel is the first in an ambitious tetralogy, a *Clan of Novels*, entitled *I Have Seen the Finger of God at Work.* The third novel in the series, published prior to the first, in 2008, is entitled *The Best Novel of All Times* and features Ceauşescu (against whose life a plot has been hatched), Swallow-Wort and other figures from the criminal underworld met in Daniel Bănulescu's previous novels.

*

Who Won the World War of Religions?—the third stage in the plan to save Romanian literature announced in Daniel Bănulescu's first volume of poems—was among sixty plays nominated for the prestigious UNITER (Theatrical Union of Romania) Award for Play of the Year in 2001. It was narrowly beaten into second place by Kincses Elemér's *The Canal*, a less spectacular, but structurally more conventional play, which explores the Hungarian and Romanian experience of forced labour under communist totalitarianism (the title refers to the Danube-Black Sea Canal, used as a means of exterminating 'enemies of the people'). Leading Romanian critic and UNITER jury member Paul Cernat, who had championed Daniel Bănulescu's play, subsequently described how the jury ultimately reached the consensus that *Who Won the World War of Religions?* was in some ways structurally wanting and suffered from "overdetermination in its stage effects." For example, some aspects of the plot, such as the arrival of the representatives of the four major religions in the mental ward setting of the play, seem inexplicable, although these fall, argues Cernat, within the conventions of the post-Beckettian theatre of the absurd. (As I shall argue below, these seeming deficiencies are in fact strengths, to be interpreted in terms of the play's eschatological vision.) Perhaps more importantly, he goes on to say, it is hard to imagine how the play might ever be staged, given the difficult challenge it would present to actors, set designers and directors. Nevertheless, Cernat concludes, the play remains a spectacular work of "dramatic literature," a "synthesis between poetry and novel," a "total work" by an author who aspires to be a "total writer".

The scene of the action for all three acts of the play remains the same: an apocalyptic ward, a "masterpiece of the madhouse setting," wherein are incarcerated twelve mental patients. The play opens on the morning of the expected arrival of a Buddhist monk, a Catholic and an Orthodox priest, and an imam, each of whom is going to attempt to persuade the patients as to the exclusive veracity of his particular religion. A brutal power struggle unfolds among the twelve mental patients, by the end of which two of them will have been killed, two reduced to the status of dogs crawling on a leash, and those remaining divided into two camps: "non-aligned" subjects and "aligned" governors, ruled over by the paranoid psychotic Waldo according to the writ of "Holy Psychiatry". At the same time, two of the four religious representatives are savagely killed by Waldo's faction, leaving the surviving two to go head to head in a contest in which each will try to disprove the other's religious doctrines. The play closes with the remaining two clerics having been bludgeoned to death in an enactment of an insane "ascension" to Heaven.

Each of the mental patients in the play is highly individualised in his own distinctive symptoms, with dramatic character being constructed according to the logic of psychopathological diagnosis. The Dramatis Personae is a series of cursory clinical records, giving the predominant psychopathological disorder for each of the twelve patients, for example, manic-depressive psychosis, aphasia, schizophrenia, paranoia, delusions of grandeur, dementia. Bănulescu in this way transfers a non-literary language into the literary discourse of the play. In this respect, the technique is the same as that employed in the third poem of the *Ballad of Daniel Bănulescu* cycle, which is made up of paediatrician's notes, written in highly technical medical terminology ("epigenetic", "hyperpnea", "phosphocalcic metabolism", etc.), alternating with longer observations, apparently written by a child psychiatrist, which ultimately form an allegory of the genesis of Daniel Bănulescu the poet: "Nurse Monica (…) notices the child humming a tune and writing—'grinning'—on a sheet of paper. She sits down next to him, tries to strike up a conversation. Met with hostility. After a while, she asks the child to show her the piece of paper. Mockingly, the child hands it to her. On the paper is written: 'Please. I'd like you to tell me. Tell me, where is your brain flying?'"

Each psychopathological note is also accompanied by a diagnosis concerning the deviations or, as it were, "diseases" of language manifest in the patients, for example, grammatical dissonance, anomalies of topic, tics, clichés. In the play itself, dramatic tension is thus created through the conflict between various language disorders—the Tourette syndrome outbursts of Olympia the cleaning woman, the seemingly structured and meaningful gibberish of Tanasîcu, "translated" by Raphael—as much as it is by conflict between characters. There is a strong sense that the languages of madness, the voices of demons, speak independently through the characters, as is the case with epileptic Virgil and the demented Kirill, whose name perhaps alludes to Kirillov in Dostoevsky's *The Demons*.

Similar to the beginning of Sartre's *Huis clos*, at the opening of the play there is brief contact with a space beyond this closed world, in the form of the cleaning woman Olympia (the name is an ironic/grotesque allusion to a higher cosmic stratum), herself quite obviously deranged, and her mute sister-in-law Vasilica, in the terminal stages of cancer, who is said to have been brought from somewhere outside. The "holies", on the other hand, are said to ascend from some lower stratum, from a cellar through a "hole in the floor": "in the cellar below us their bodies jolted (…) they have been waiting for hundreds of years." Through a series of hints and allusions the impression is created of a stratified hell, as when Caius says, "Before we can at last live in Paradise, we must first traverse the barriers of devils above us." The very stage set and props of the play also provide a strong eschatological intimation. The disarray, heteroclite junk and detritus are reminiscent of the underworld visited by Epistemon in Chapter Thirty of Rabelais' *Pantagruel*, where once mighty kings are reduced to the scurvy condition of patchers and pot-scrapers. In the Third Act, when the curtain rises to reveal Orthodox priest Paranasius bound and thrust inside a huge cauldron of soiled sheets and Muslim imam Zaid inside a metal tank for dirty dishes and leftovers, the image may therefore be placed within a tradition of grotesque hells that stretches from Aristophanes (the "river of shit and mud" in *The Frogs*) and Lucian of Samosata (*Dialogi Inferorum*) down through Rabelais and later Menippean satire. Likewise analogous are the infernal enclosed spaces crammed with dilapidated junk described in the proto-surreal, proto-absurd writings of Urmuz (1883-1923), where we find old rags, cracked plates, rusty funnels, punctured cooking oil canisters, broken piano lids, perished rubber bladders, etc.

There are also frequent eschatological intimations in the dialogue between the characters. In an early exchange between Olympia and Pica ('pica' is a disorder characterised by the ingestion of non-nutritive substances, such as soil, soap, faeces, or metal objects etc.), Olympia alludes to the patients having once been buried by gravediggers, but Pica says they escaped from the graveyard. She says that their hovel is built "over a devil's backside"—in the literature and iconography of the eschatological grotesque the underworld is frequently conceived as being a fundament, and in their sparring Waldo and Paranasius repeatedly use the appellative "Bowel of Hell". Elsewhere, reference is made to a jug of gold coins stashed under shit-stained sheets, which can be interpreted as a scatological allusion to the Gospel parable of the unprofitable servant who buries the talent his Lord gives him rather than using it to gain more talents, and is thus cast into the outer darkness, where there is weeping and wailing and gnashing of teeth: "For unto every one that hath shall be given, and he shall have abundance: but from him that hath not shall be taken away even that which he hath" (Matthew, 30: 29). The head of the king on the coin buried by the unprofitable servant is a symbol of the image and likeness of God, its burial the attempt to reject God and hide from Him. In the play, the gold coins are said to bear the image of "an emperor with a great big jaw": in hell, the damned are incapable of imagining God except in terms of fear, hatred and derision. There are also intimations of infernal torments, inflicted by unseen and unnamed persecutors, as when Pica says, "yesterday, when they pulled our guts out and thrashed them with a stick." Similarly, Caius remarks, "each and every one of us feels as though, every ten minutes, he has been snatched away by a host of devils. Beaten until he vomits blood. Then put back unnoticed." Otherwise, the damned are tormented by their inner demons, or else they torment each other—*l'enfer c'est les autres*.

The faction of the tormentors forms a hierarchy with the paranoid and sadistic Waldo at its head. Waldo, having eliminated his rival, Tanasîcu, establishes himself as a kind of God, dwelling in the onstage tent marked "Heaven", with Holy Psychiatry in the hypostasis of the Holy Ghost, speaking through the medical prophets of his psychiatric textbook. Waldo's ministering angels, the "governors" of this psychiatric hell, are apparelled in a slipshod parody of medical and ecclesiastical authority, with vestments from the murdered and the captive clerics covering their tattered, filthy mental-patient pyjamas. The torments they inflict are alternately a grotesque parody of religious ministration, as in the climactic scene of Act Two, in which the language of exorcism is wielded by the possessed (Kirill), and of medical care, in which the language of psychiatry is applied by the mentally ill. As the monkey is a mockery of man, so too demons are a mockery of angels.

The "Festival of Meetings", in which representatives of Buddhism, Orthodox Christianity, Roman-Catholicism, and Islam each vie to convince the twelve mental patients of the exclusive truth of his own religion, can be interpreted as a grotesque parody of the theological *disputatio* between, for example, a Christian, a philosopher, and a Jew, which was a genre common in mediaeval times. As well as being a literary-theological genre, such disputations actually took place, often with high political stakes. One famous example was the theological disputation that was held by Prince Vladimir in Kiev in the year 988 and attended by representatives of all the "Abrahamic" monotheistic religions—Judaism, Orthodoxy, Catholicism and Islam—as a result of which Orthodoxy became the state religion of Russia, as it has remained for more than a thousand years, excepting the seven decades of Soviet rule. Romanian cultural anthropologist Andrei Oişteanu has collected more than seventy-five historical instances of such public theological disputations, ranging from Iceland in the west as far as Japan in the east. In *Who Won the World War of Religions?* the disputation is framed grotesquely in sporting terms, with the murderous lunatics who are in charge of the asylum providing a running commentary that parodies that of a tennis or football match. After the elimination of Ignatius, the Catholic priest, bludgeoned over the head with iron bars, it becomes clear that this will be a match to the death. The semi-final and final, which take the form of a question-and-answer session between the three surviving contestants, might also be read as an infernal parody of a televised election debate between party-political leaders. Elsewhere, the link between hell and politics is also made explicit when the voices that speak through the epileptic Virgil describe themselves as "an occupying regime", a "mass demonstration".

Who, in the end, wins the World War of Religions? The answer, in the play, would seem to be no one, or at least none of those present. Shortly before the "governors" deal the death blow to Paranasius and Zaid, Caius says, "The religions not only do not destroy the devils, but behind the scenes, the religions and the devils passionately kiss," to which Raphael, the erstwhile interpreter of the murdered Tanasîcu, rejoins, "Not all religions…" The key to the play, however, is a theodicy, a vindication of the existence of God by virtue of the existence of evil. God is absent because hell is the absence of God. The existence of hell, as the absence of God, is therefore proof of the existence of God. When Zaid asks the Buddhist Amanda, "Does God exist?" Pica interjects, "How could He not? Otherwise what are we all doing here?" For the damned, hell is thus precisely abandonment and the absence of God, as when Caius, before withdrawing into the "Government" tent at the end of the play, says, "We're covered in illness, suffering, death and devils, like an abandoned table covered with dust." The image is reminiscent of the image of eternity as a dark country bathhouse with cobwebs in the corners which the godless Svidrigailov describes to the horrified Raskolnikov in *Crime and Punishment*. But in the end, even in the depths of hell and the absence of God, there is a glimmer of messianic hope: Raphael, "translating" the stuttering words of Pica, who reports what a friend had once read to him from a book, tells the patients left on stage, after the withdrawal of the demonised conspirators, the words of "Jehovah God" to man: "Behold. Soon I come."

Bibliography

Te voi iubi pîn' la sfîrșitul patului (*I'll Love You to the End of the Bed*), Cartea Românească: Bucharest, 1993

Te pup în fund, Conducător iubit! (*I Kiss Your Arse, Beloved Leader!*), Editura Nemira: Bucharest, 1994

Balada lui Daniel Bănulescu (*culeasă și prelucrată de el însuși*) *The Ballad of Daniel Bănulescu* (*Picked and Fashioned by Himself*), Cartea Românească: Bucharest, 1997.

Cei șapte regi ai orașului București (*The Seven Kings of the City of Bucharest*), Editura Nemira: Bucharest, 1998

Republica Federală Daniel Bănulescu. Statul de nord & Statul de sud (*The Federal Republic of Daniel Bănulescu. Northern State and Southern State*), ed. Nicolae Țone, Editura Vinea: Bucharest, 2000

Daniel, al rugăciunii (*prima jumătate a anului*) *Daniel, of the Prayer* (*The First Half of the Year*), Editura Muzeul Literaturii Române: Bucharest, 2002

Schrumpeln wirst du wirst eine exotische Frucht sein, trans. Ernst Wichner, Edition per procura: Vienna, 2003

Ich küsse dir den Hintern, Geliebter Führer! trans. Anca Munteanu, Edition per procura: Vienna, 2005

Cel mai bun roman al tuturor timpurilor (*The Best Novel of All Time*), Cartea Românească: Bucharest, 2008

Fugi din viața ta, revoltătoare și slută, în cartea mea (*Flee from Your Revolting and Hideous Life into My Book*), Cartea Românească: Bucharest, 2009

Ce bine e să fii Daniel Bănulescu (*How Good it is to be Daniel Bănulescu*), Cartea Românească: Bucharest, 2010

Daniel Bănulescu

WHO WON THE WORLD WAR OF RELIGIONS?

A Play in Three Acts

DRAMATIS PERSONAE

OLYMPIA The cleaning woman. Fifty years old. Employed by the hospital for nervous illnesses. She cleans the ward in which twelve special patients are isolated.

VASILICA Olympia's sister-in-law. Thirty-five years old. Mute. Brought to visit from outside the ward.

MARCEL Patient number 1. Preponderant illness: perceptional disturbances; hallucinations. He "nurtures" at his breast a baby made out of scraps of rag. (Soft, somewhat feminine. Unexpectedly lubricious. Often naïve. A gossip. Without any grammatical dissonances.)

PICA Patient number 2. Preponderant illness: polyphagy; disturbances of instinctual behaviour; alimentary aberrations. (General culinary interest. A kind of third in command within the group, he sometimes arbitrates disputes. Generally non-violent, "well-intentioned". Serious grammatical dissonances. Unravelling of sentence topic.)

LUPU Patient number 3. Preponderant illness: corporeal hallucinations – he believes he has been metamorphosed into a wolf. Former history teacher. (Howls and has a lupine "consciousness". He speaks in a perfectly academic fashion, supplying odd historical facts, many of them exact. He knits together exact information and aberrations.)

THE PRINCE Patient number 4. Preponderant illness: mythomania; pathological lying; cognitive disturbances. (Conduit of fear: "What if they find me?" Because of this a certain suicidal tendency. Grammatically correct. Inappropriately ceremonious and precious verbal expression. Interminable sentences.)

TANASÎCU Patient number 5. Preponderant illness: aphasia; behavioural disturbances. Leader number 1 of the "tribe" of patients, at least for the moment. His utterances, generally unintelligible, are "translated" for the others by his friend, Raphael. (Grammatically unstructured language, but meaningful. Sometimes tics.)

GEORGE Patient number 6. Preponderant illness: alcoholism; state of confusion; delirium tremens. He drinks anything at all: spirit, petrol, toothpaste mixed with water. In the absence of such substances, he continuously sucks a handkerchief in order to assuage his suffering. (Trembling. Excitement. He resorts to theft, begging, blackmail, etc. Obscenity, vulgarity. Rarely, ideas of jealousy, or else he speaks of himself in the third person. Pronounced grammatical dissonances. Verbal tics.)

RAPHAEL Patient number 7. Preponderant illness: manic-depressive psychosis; the malady attacks the sphere of activity cyclically: a) maniacal episode and b) depressive episode. He is the friend and protector of Tanasîcu, translating for others what Tanasîcu wishes to communicate. Otherwise, he very rarely involves himself in discussions. (Clean. Sensitive. Friendly. Shy and naïve. During depressive episodes, he obsessively attempts suicide. Particularly correct grammatical expression.)

CAIUS Patient number 8. Preponderant illness: schizophrenia; discordance between feelings and reactions; affective ambivalence. He is "the one who (almost always) poses questions". Bizarre behaviour. Morbid rationalism. Active in discussions. However, when he himself is asked a question, he answers beside the point, "obliquely". (Extremely impressionable. Unjustifiably cruel or kind. Collects garbage. Sometimes talks to himself. Illogical. Almost grammatically correct. Rare grammatical dissonances.)

WALDO Patient number 9. Preponderant illness: paranoia; systematic delusions of grandeur, persecution, jealousy. Impervious to criticism. Megalomania. At the outset, he is second in command within the ward, in tacit and mortal conflict with Tanasîcu. He reads to his fellow patients their supposed diagnoses from a psychiatry book hidden under his mattress. (Extremely cunning and resentful. Logical. Skilful. He is capable of anything; he will play any kind of role. He speaks correctly, sometimes even academically. The crafted hairpin bends of his sentences bode derision. Preponderantly short sentences.)

KIRILL Patient number 10. Preponderant illness: dementia. He is a "sick man who has been ruined". Progressive and irreversible decline in affectivity. (He speaks in snatches of slogans and commonplaces, which fit like a square peg in a round hole. Sphincteral incontinence. Gradual loss of self-awareness. "Senile scars" are spreading over his cerebral cortex. Stereotypes of the "Be a nice lady. Don't make mincemeat of me" kind.)

ZOLI Patient number 11. Preponderant illness: oligophrenia. The oligophrenic is a "sick man who was born and dies poor". Deficient psychical development, cerebral lesions, character showing the after-effects. Vegetative existence. (Most often, his communication consists of inarticulate screams to signal essential biological necessities. He watches over the other patients. Sometimes, however, he makes surprising interruptions with songs and poems whose meaning he obviously does not perceive.)

VIRGIL Patient number 12. Preponderant illness: epilepsy. Unconscious rhythmic and violent movements, sudden loss of consciousness, accompanied by falling, foaming at the mouth, tongue-biting etc. Exaggerated emotional instability, going from states of exaggerated gaiety to depression. (Preponderantly amiable. In appearance, the least subject to the influence of the ward leaders. Friendly. Open. Cheerful. But sudden deteriorations in mood. Despair. Jealousy. Attempts at suicide. Epileptic fits perhaps a means of discharging an emotional state. Average intelligence. Manipulated with extreme ease. Almost grammatically correct. Banal in expression, without marked particularities.)

PARANASIUS Believer in the teachings of the Eastern Christian Orthodox Church. Priest of that Church. Man of very advanced years. He is garbed in a surplice, highly ceremonial priestly vestments, stitched with gold and silver thread. Over his surplice and stole, a large gold cross hangs from his neck. He has a censer and icon to hand. He wears a long, white beard.

IGNATIUS Believer in the teachings of the Roman-Catholic Church. (Celibate) priest of that church. Man of very advanced years. Dressed wholly in black vestments. A medallion with a gold cross hangs at his chest. Hair cropped short, shaven cheeks.

AMANDA Believer in the teachings of Buddha. Member of a Buddhist monastic order. Among the monks of this order, he has the highest rank, that of "archate", which means "saint", or "released while still in life". Man of very advanced years. He wears the voluminous yellow robe of a mendicant monk. Apart from this robe, he owns only a girdle, a bowl for food given as alms, a sieve, and a needle. His scalp and cheeks are shaven.

ZAID Believer in the teachings of Islam. Given that there is no priesthood as this is understood in other religions, Zaid is an "imam", or "prayer leader". During ritual prayers, the imam sits in front of the other worshippers, who call themselves "Muslims", or "those who submit". The Muslims form rows behind the imam and, in order not to make any mistake, repeat his words and gestures exactly. A man of very advanced years. He is dressed in flowing white robes, and wears a turban on his head. He has a moustache, but apart from that his cheeks are shaven. On the right hand side of his girdle hangs a curved dagger, housed in a sheath.

ACT ONE

SET AND PRELIMINARIES

A masterpiece of the madhouse setting. Inside the hospital ward can be found: twelve beds; twelve nightstands; other categories of furniture, made of sturdy materials and fastened to the floor or walls; and wheelchairs.

Disarray. Remnants of hospital supplies and medical apparatus.

As you look towards the stage, you can see:

Six beds plus six nightstands along the left-hand wall.

The other six beds plus remaining nightstands along the wall at the back of the stage.

Along the right-hand wall: two immense windows, crisscrossed by barbed wire and bars. Beneath the window (beginning at the back of the stage): a toilet (consisting of holes in the floor with cast iron footrests to either side, and a few chamber pots); locked metal filing cabinets; a huge table and – pushed underneath and leaning against the wall – a bench of the same length; a cauldron with a heap of dirty sheets; a sink; a massive box (in which leftovers, spoons, and dishes are usually deposited); and lastly a metal door, framed by another two doors made of meshes of soldered barbed wire.

In the middle of the ward: jumble (wheelchairs, bunched-up sheets, broken objects), and a free space.

At the beginning of the play, the twelve patients are sitting dispersed on their beds. They give the impression of having been interrupted in a heated argument. They gaze fixedly at the first person to enter, Olympia *the cleaning woman, and are unanimous in a reaction that is half terror, half mockery.*

As events unfold, the patients will form two or more conflicting groups, grouped around the leaders of opinion at any given time. The two initial leaders do not at all conceal their hatred towards each other. They are Tanasîcu *and* Waldo.

The clanking of the door being unlocked.

The imposing cleaning woman, Olympia, *enters the room. The metal doors are locked behind her and her companion.*

She rushes into the middle of the room like a tempest. Olympia *is laden with primitive cleaning implements. Broom-, brush- and mop-handles bristle from her back, making her look like a hedgehog.*

In general, Olympia *will act, according to the principle of repose alternating with exaggeratedly rhythmic action, like a hen.*

This is how: she suddenly hurls to the floor the mountains of baggage she has carted behind her into the ward; she remains motionless; then she rushes to the mound of sheets in the cauldron, in whose innards she rummages with her arms, then with the sabre of a brush, looking for something which, it seems, she does not find; once again she becomes motionless. She is thinking resolutely about the next area into which she is going to rush and rummage.

By the metal doors (having entered the ward at the same time as Olympia*), a second, younger woman has remained –* Vasilica. Vasilica *is abnormally ill at ease. She continually twists the corners of her blouse in embarrassment. No one pays any attention to her.*

All twelve pairs of inmate eyes in the ward blink, gape in alarm, or wink mockingly depending on the place where Olympia *is or is not rummaging.*

Olympia *is scrabbling with a hook behind the filing cabinets. Then she remains motionless, emitting her characteristic moos of desolation. She unexpectedly thrusts herself under* Marcel's *bed. Nothing. But she does not forget to release the proper onomatopoeia of disappointment.*

In the end, Olympia *resorts to the only method never yet to have failed: visual and verbal examination of each patient. The woman stations herself in the geometric centre of the room. She plants her palms on her hips and her gaze on the pupils of each of the twelve patients.*

OLYMPIA (*after ferociously examining two patients*): Where is it?

TANASÎCU (*quickly intervening, in the fear that one of his fellow inmates might unpredictably betray him, as in fact happens every morning*): BIRBAZIMO CHEKA?

OLYMPIA (*for a moment disconcerted*): Eh? ...

RAPHAEL (*naïve, serene, brimming with amiableness. Obviously, he is doing no more than "translating" the aphasic replies, unintelligible to the others, barked by* Tanasîcu): He says what is it to be?

TANASÎCU (*barking*): HUP HUPA?

RAPHAEL ("translating" candidly): He says that why are you poking your nose in?

OLYMPIA: Aha! …So why should I sticks me nose in…gentlemen they woken up today with their willies a wee bit stiff and they wants to get up to some hanky-panky. Spoiling for a scrap they is… (*Stops rummaging, stands hands on hips, mimicking amazement*) Well now, the very first stiffy you lot ever got was in the graveyard!

PICA: We escaped from here! …Who are you asking, why you can't find your graveyard, if we were escaped from here a long time ago?!

TANASÎCU: BANAVATAGINTA!

RAPHAEL (respectfully enunciating everything required to "translate" Tanasîcu's replies): You cow!

OLYMPIA (she has resumed her rummaging with even greater fury): Arse! (*Unexpectedly, she stands up straight and takes a menacing step towards the patients*) You're dead and buried! If them injections weren't running through you like water through a tap, the gravediggers would swear you were nowt but twelve bits of monkey, hacked up by a sawmill. (*She becomes pensive.*) Or not even monkeys… 'Cause even monkeys… There's monkeys and there's monkeys… Some has ones thicker than a horse's…
(*She changes her strategy. She tries the kindly aunt treatment, looking at each of them with something like a smile and sweetening her tone.*) Come on and confess to auntie Olympia… If you've ever tousled… For real. A woman's brush?!

GEORGE (he extracts his moistened handkerchief from his mouth. He is trying to insult Olympia and, in desperation at not finding anything sufficiently offensive, he incorrectly mimics Tanasîcu's previous cry): You banavagica!

OLYMPIA: Eh?!... Did you see that?!... I mean, how could you do any tousling?! Who's the dirty woman that'd let you? …'Cause these nutters they is all chained up in their ward. She'd see the man's 'jamas… She'd recognise the bodywork… But when it came to… She'd be better off sticking her finger up her arse. (*She changes the game yet again, rummaging feverishly. Pausing. Lifting her head. And with the same booming bellow with which she entered the stage asking*): Where the devil is it?

THE PRINCE (*in order to distract her attention, rises from the white metal chair on which he has been lolling, between his bed and his nightstand. He manages the tour-de-force of maintaining a dignified appearance even in the ragged pyjamas that hang from him. He greets Olympia with a slight inclination of the chin. He speaks to her, referring to the person with whom she has entered the ward, who has remained by the door, in the penumbra*): Aren't you going to introduce us?

OLYMPIA (*after barely refraining from cursing him or hitting him, her eyes flash with irony*): Excuse me. (*She fetches her companion and plants her in the middle of the room.*) This sluggard is our Vasilica, me sister-in-law, a treasure… A good lass… Stays quiet where you puts her. She's mute. (In a chatty tone, in line with the sympathy she senses Vasilica has stirred among the inmates): Six months back, don't know how, she wound up with breast cancer… A month back, she weren't careful and got blood poisoning. Got threads growing in her…

CAIUS (*serious; not understanding the significance of what he has heard*): Very nice. Blood threads on top of threads and one night you find you have a brand new woollen blanket… No?!

OLYMPIA: …T'other day, a hepatic cirrhosis come and bore an hole in her liver. Big enough to fit a bag of sunflower seeds in there…

PICA (*instantly, jumping up hungrily*): I want some sunflower seeds too!

(*Miraculously, this is just what happens. While Olympia resumes her disclosures about her sister-in-law's infirmities, Vasilica silently goes over to Pica's bed. From her pocket she removes a paper cornet of sunflower seeds. And she mutely pours them into Pica's cupped palms.*)

PICA (*although overwhelmed by emotion, he does not miss the opportunity to devour them in a single gulp. Then he wipes his mouth. Tardily, he adds, with residual imploring*): …At least two…

OLYMPIA: …Her kidney done rotted. Her eyes gone dim. Falls on the stairs. Not even that blanket is any great shakes. 'Cause she spits up the blood and the threads… So I says to myself, rather than pay her gravediggers and all, better I lets her sweep up and clean the turds in them lot's ward, until she gets better. *(To Vasilica)*: Oi, just wash, don't sweep as well! Don't get completely better… (Turning once more to the patients. With a mysterious, complicit tone): Where did you stash it this time?

TANASÎCU (threateningly): SIK CHAK PANASIKA!

OLYMPIA (imitating him and seeking to follow all the clues it seems she can detect in Tanasîcu's cry): Sik Chak Panasika… He's saying the only proper hidy-hole you found is under the sink?

RAPHAEL: No. Tanasîcu says that you must be completely mad if, every morning, you keep doing our heads in with your stupid questions about the sink. And that given you haven't proven capable of being appointed anything but broom-lady over our ward…

OLYMPIA: Me, a broom-lady?!

MARCEL (with bonhomie, cradling his rag "baby"): You're not going to turn into a pianist, are you?!

OLYMPIA: Me! Keep flaying you with questions about the sink?

MARCEL: Every which way. As if we didn't suspect who it is that keeps blocking your air vent with fingernails, hairballs, perfusion tubes, bandages, cockroaches.

CAIUS (explanatory, trying to help): The cockroaches that block your sink are hauled from other wards on the backs of other cockroaches.

PICA: …And the bandages, which caused the flooding, were fetched in the mouths of other bandages.

OLYMPIA: Arrgh! I hope you get struck down by electric shocks… Listen to them! The cockroaches dragged the bandages in their mouths, did they… What nasty folk!

MARCEL: That's the way it is. There couldn't be folk nastier.

PICA: There's no way you can change them.

OLYMPIA: As if they didn't have any idea about what needs howking out. They pretend I'm wagging me tongue for nowt. But that witchery with the wages, pinched a year back, from the director's office, and when I goes to look for them. They turn up again, seven days ago, under *Zoli's* mattress… Was it him who towed all the bandages here in his gob too?

TANASÎCU: BABARDAMINA DILCO!

OLYMPIA: Comely bandages! He worked hard Thursday. But he got up at the crack of dawn on Friday too… Wasn't it me who found here… six days ago, under the mound of shit-stained sheets, a great big jug, bursting with gold coins, minted at the orders of some emperor. One with a great big jaw… You could feel it just by fingering the face chiselled on them…

TANASÎCU: DIDISALAZANO HALALA!

OLYMPIA: …Of course, he had a halala a thousand times more first-class than your weenies. (*Rummaging, sweeping and cleaning the wall with detergent, she continues to advance deeper into the ward, and is about to reach the area of the sink. Behind her, Vasilica assists, staring at the floor and cleaning conscientiously.*) Otherwise, you wouldn't have turned out so wonky… That's why I'm saying… Five days ago, tidying in the attic and brushing the cobwebs off them new apparatuses… Didn't *Olympia* find a great big silver spear stuck in the panel with buttons?! … (*With her voice at the same volume, she speaks as though to herself*): One of those ones King Decebal of Dacia played with when he got bored. And when he got bored he'd run off to give Mrs Decebal a good seeing to, and 'cause of that she gave birth to loads of poisoned bairns… 'Cause Decebal always had marks from that silver spear on his hands… (*She directs her entire attention towards the patients once more*): Isn't that right, mouldy stinkers?

(*The patients maintain a disengaging silence. After a few seconds, Pica intervenes, however, speaking completely obliquely to what has been under discussion up to now. His phrasing is convincing, as though he were imparting to the others from the mineral deposits of his wisdom.*)

PICA: If you don't teach potatoes to gobble up the meat when they're young, you'll never be able to make a stew with weevils in it.

LUPU (*without any particular enthusiasm, gets out of bed on all fours and emits lupine howls*): Ooo-oo! …Ooo-oo! …Ooo-oo!

OLYMPIA: …On Sunday, behind that knackered scran trolley, what does auntie Olympia find but a great big pile of books bound in calfskin, all scribbled on by some drunks. 'Cause not even with a helping hand from the devil could you figure out what those alcoholics thought they'd written in them!

GEORGE (*removes the handkerchief from his mouth, speaks, and then stuffs his hanky-dummy back in again*): She finds. Bugger them alcoholics 'cause she finds.

OLYMPIA: There's squads of soldiers thick as bunches of grapes to guard this devils' ward of yours. Where, once you've stayed two days, the only thing left for you to do is to give your mother a thrashing with the crutches you arrived on. In this ward where the only ones they don't cure are you, that's what devils you are. Or am I wrong?! (*To Lupu*): What's it say in your history book, prof?

MARCEL: Say. It's not healthy to teach children to kill their mothers with crutches.

PICA: I've told you already that we were escaped out of here. Why doesn't she ask the potatoes?

OLYMPIA: …Yesterday morning, I come into the ward and a glass snail, six feet tall. Plip, plop… Dragging itself across the floor. It were banging a drum around its neck and croaking: "Repent!! …'Cause if you don't repent now, then today or tomorrow… The devil knows what will happen to you! …"

VIRGIL: Repent, then! Don't mess with a snail!

OLYMPIA: My arse. What can happen to us?! Look, nothing's happened to me… And today… What nasty folk! …Arrgh! You'll find that those herds of cockroaches have been sent to happen to us by that wretched snail.

(*Indeed, in the area around the sink, on a visible portion of the wall, an impressive colony of cockroaches is teeming. As quick as lightning, Mrs Olympia whips off her left slipper and skilfully squashes three of the insects against the plaster.*)

GEORGE: They isn't cockroaches. They's pearls.

CAIUS: They're neither pearls nor cockroaches. They're precious stones.

WALDO (*authoritarian and honeyed, he takes stock and ticks off, in a notebook, the first targets attained by the exterminator of insects. In a previous understanding between the inmates, each cockroach on the wall has been given a number, corresponding to the number of each patient's bed*): Three… nine… eleven… The others, whose cockroaches haven't been squashed, are to come to our beds, the winners' beds, by tomorrow, each with 200 grams of fresh bread.

OLYMPIA (*with a certain consideration towards Waldo*): See I don't whack 200 grams of broom handle over your back, so that you'll swear I've served you restaurant food. (*Addressing them all*): This hovel of yours, with all your tricks, must have been built over the hole in a devil's backside. You only have to wiggle a bit and out of some crack all them cockroaches swarm on top of you like devils.

VASILICA (*pointing at the mound with the cockroaches*): Mmph! …Mmph! …Mmph!

PICA: They isn't cockroaches. They's pearls.

MARCEL: *Vasilica* saw them first. *Vasilica* is the Virgin Mary!

OLYMPIA: I hope your eyes split in four! A thirty-stone Virgin Mary, rotting alive. With two-feet tumours along her bones, and at home, five brats waiting for her swimming in their own snot.

CAIUS: They aren't brats. They're cockroaches.

THE PRINCE: Back in the days when I knew her, on my honour, she was a sparkling doll, with a waist no thicker than a biscuit, and most willing to lose her mind whenever me met… Five years ago, I was rubbing the numb tendons of a light bay stallion, on the riding tracks of an estate, which I had given to a devotee of mine… And this accursed *Vasilica* was the only one who dared to lift her eyes from the ground in those ten minutes after I had passed by that place. Well, as I was saying, one morning…

WALDO: We know. You shit yourself.

THE PRINCE (*crushed and petrified, he tries to conceal the fear Waldo inspires in him*): I think that this is a malicious interpretation… I admit… that, from hill to hill, my bay horse left droppings…

OLYMPIA (*overwhelmed by the continual inundation of insects*): Eek! Look! …You'll find that we'll not be repenting for nowt, like that thieving snail advised! …Today, it must be the not the cockroaches' but precious stones' turn to come out of the cracks…

PICA: Ha!

GEORGE (*his constant gesture: the handkerchief pulled out, with hatred, a riposte, the handkerchief put back in the mouth to be sucked*): No it's not!

OLYMPIA: Ahaaa! Bandy-legged nun! …Crawling with cockroaches! … This isn't no cockroach cockroach, this is a precious-stone cockroach! (*She twists the pleats of her dress around so that she can reach into a side pocket. She fishes out a rag pouch. She picks bits of the strange treasure off the plaster and stuffs them in the pouch.*) And this is a precious-stone cockroach too, except that it's a precious-stone cockroach splatted by a slipper! …And a precious stone on the bulgy bit! …And over the plaster scurry the poor precious stones, like they was bringing back a herd of pigs from the pasture! There you are, greasers. And precious stones… back to the sty! …*Vasilica*, move your arse-cheeks, and pen them all in for me… And you nutcases, you're still going to get nowt but a stew of rotten plums to chew on when you're hungry! If you'll allow me, I'm going to kidnap the Virgin Mary for a little, so she can buff the precious stones in my office. Out you go, lass!

(*The two women leave the ward.*)

PICA (*speaking to her back as Olympia leaves the room*): You don't swallow mine, but don't you give me yours to swallow either! …Pointless you trying to leave the ward with them, same as in all the other years, as soon as you set foot outside your treasures will still turn to ash… And when you suck up to us… with aaah (*he salivates*) …warm bread, toasted peanuts and… ah… cheese… Then we… (*salivates copiously*) …no! Then, I'm going to munch your liver!

LUPU: She has no liver!

KIRILL: We'll all tuck into some liver.

GEORGE (*the usual fuss with the hanky*): Yes. We'll all drink our livers away!

(*A few moments of silence settle. The patients resume the conversation which was presumably interrupted when Olympia burst into the ward with Vasilica in tow, at the beginning of the play.*)

VIRGIL: Me, if he doesn't move my table. At least from the filing cabinets as far as the windows… He can bang his head against the walls for all I care. I still won't believe him!

MARCEL: How could he move it!? …Have you forgotten when they brought us it and they plonked it down through the window with three cranes, how their necks were straining, like they had been soldered with chewing gum?! And as soon as they got it down, how they fixed it to the floor with hinges as big as your leg!? With screws as big as melons!? And bolts removed from the coffins of the drowned using a patent!?

GEORGE (*the gesture with the handkerchief*): The drowned have got bolts, if you stick your cock in them, however soft it'll get broke!

CAIUS: But how could that Catholic lift the table up in the air, like a sparrow? …And when he got bored making it like a sparrow, he got it to wipe all the spider webs in each corner of the ceiling, like a duster.

WALDO: He wasn't a Catholic. He was a Hindu. And Hindus are initiated into the flying table trick as soon as they're born… They start to walk… And they're taken to have their first piddle in their holy river, the Ganges by name.

GEORGE (*the handkerchief gesture*): They tempt him with it being holy, but he pisses in it.

KIRILL: Bravo! That's the way.

WALDO: They walk into the river until it's up to their knees… They piously undo the braces of their short trousers. They reverently unfasten their zip… And they let rip into the Ganges with their first hot and damp prayer.

LUPU (*pauses in one of his agitated walks on all fours diagonally across the ward. He lifts his chin in Waldo's direction, as though he were listening to one of the "voices" only he can hear. As he listens to the "voice", Lupu's tormented face, that of a beast terrorised by an itch, intermittently acquires a human expression, still tormented, but coaxed into sharing his knowledge*): Hindu pups – Ooo-oo! – don't wear short trousers… Their garb doesn't permit them short trousers. The Hindus go around wearing long pieces of cloth. With one free corner thrown over the shoulder, called a sari. Ever since their ancestors met with a pack of wolves, friends of mine, and those wolves ripped their braces!

CAIUS: But if you say that wolves are so clever, why don't they teach those… errr… I forget what you call them… Why don't they teach those what-do-you-call-them to build nests, like sparrows?

THE PRINCE (as though catching the idea): Orthodox believers?

CAIUS: Exactly.

VIRGIL: Ha, ha, ha. I'm telling you absolutely for certain. Sparrows never build nests.

MARCEL (continues to busy himself with the rag baby he keeps at his chest. After he has rocked it, cradling it now in his right, now in his left arm, he finally settles it in his lap. He removes the piece of cloth that is supposed to protect the "baby's breathing". He lovingly strokes what is supposed to be the baby's "little face". He puts back the cloth to protect the baby's breathing. He settles the rag doll in his lap once more, all the while conversing with the other patients in the ward.): Wait a minute! Let me stop the little one's ears. So that who knows what blasphemy won't make its nest in his little head.

PICA (discontent, but speaking more to himself, with reference to the "baby" which, although Marcel has got it ready for bed, the same Marcel has neglected to feed): You wouldn't even put a dog to bed without feeding it some bricks first…

MARCEL (his maternal ministrations having come to a close): Now tell him… *(He has a candour and non-aggressive directness that characterises almost every action.)* So, the sparrows have it off standing up, for all to see. Without caring either whom or whom they get pregnant?!

WALDO (not missing the opportunity to attack him, using a venomous and cloying tone): I bet our Orthodox won't be too happy when he finds out about how you suggested that he has it off standing up, for all to see…

CAIUS (finding himself contradicting Waldo, but only half-heartedly, it is true):

It's not like he was suggesting…

PICA (*sincerely*): He didn't suggest it… But it wouldn't have gone amiss to fill his belly with something.

WALDO (*not seeming to care overly much about Pica or Caius. He has fixed his sights on his prey. He speaks to Marcel in particular*): I can almost see him – not long from now, when the four kinds of holies once more ascend from the cellars, to unfold their miracles directly among you. I can almost see our stormy Orthodox priest – nasally chanting his unintelligible sermons – I can almost see him shaking his fist and gnashing his teeth as soon as he finds out what you said about him. No one has any idea how crafty he is at whacking you with his icon on the sly, while around the four holy men your wave of implorations for healing swells.

MARCEL (*ingenuous, reversing the situation*): And why should you implore him, dear Waldo, if that Orthodox priest will prove to be so insufferable? …Do you know what? Ignore him… When you see him coming to beg you to implore him. Quickly turn your back and nicely ask him to kiss your bottom… But why is it that you, Waldo, are thinking of imploring him? (*For a few moments, profound wonderment.*) …Could it be that, without complaining of anything to anyone, you're very ill!?

VIRGIL (*so amused at the comical situation that it no longer even crosses his mind that he should be afraid of Waldo*): Ha! Ha! Ha! …The old fox kept trying to fit the rabbit on the spit. But in the end, the rabbit, ten times cleverer, had skewered the fox and was already roasting him… (*Amicably, to Waldo, pointing at Marcel*): He doesn't hit the mark that often, but sometimes he succeeds.

WALDO (*dryly, directing his fury at Virgil*): As for me, in your place, I'd be better off thinking about your wife's difficult temperament! You languish here, feeble, in hospital, and poor *Claudia* is forced to relieve her female urges with even the dustbin men who unblock the rubbish chutes in blocks of flats! With the blokes from the next block, because she's already worn out all the ones in your block… How much the delicate and capricious *Claudia* has to put up with, just so that she won't miss an opportunity with a wearer of longjohns! …She's like a poll tax on this country. How many things has she not whispered to me so that, after impaling her on my stake, she might convince me to grill her on the spit a little longer! …Look, don't you want, at least just this once, to prove you're a man? …Close your eyes! …Listen only to me! …Count to three… Have you closed them?

PICA (*circumspectly*): Don't close them. Who knows what revolting doctor will turn up here and gobble them up.

KIRILL (*muttering something, without showing that he has been taking any notice of anyone*): If we die and we get bored, wake us up!

VIRGIL (*halfway through Virgil's tirade, begins to rock back and forth imperceptibly and has the urge to stick his fingers in his ears. He represses this tendency. He even tries to put on a smile. He does not succeed. Then he gives his answer, writhing*): Leave me alone! …You don't know her! … If I hadn't been the one to tell you something about my marriage… one evening, you wouldn't have heard of her in any of your sinful lives!

WALDO: Very well! Maybe I'm mistaken and she didn't whisper anything to me. But have you closed them? …Close them, sir. Good! …Now relax…

PICA: Don't relax!

WALDO (*continuing to speak only to Virgil, without paying any attention to Pica*): Now start counting… Five… Nine… Eleven… Seventeen… Visualise them… Don't peek! …Play fairly! …Seventeen dustbin men, lumberjacks, and unskilled manual labourers from the compressor factory are queuing up along the landing, along the hall, the living room, as far as the door handle of a little room at the end of the corridor… The hulking fellows are yawning, scratching themselves, trying to articulate the words from a sporting gazette, swigging from the bottle of vodka by their feet… Waiting impatiently to get to the bedroom… Whose door occasionally opens… And the wispy voice of your wife invites them, one by one, inside… To show them all your wedding photographs! … (*Observing that he has finished off his victim, he adds, to himself*): Claudia! I don't think I've ever met a woman with such a name.

(*In the meantime, Virgil has continued to rock back and forth, he has given a first shout, and his throat is rattling. From this moment, his state will gradually and implacably alter. As though someone had lit a long fuse. Virgil will slowly slide from a state of unmotivated jollity to apathy, from apathy to melancholy, from melancholy to sadness. Sadness will be replaced by the blackest depression. In these latter stages of affectivity, his gaze will become more and more fixed, his eyes more and more bloodshot.*)

TANASÎCU (*commandingly and threateningly, to Waldo*): BIC SART TIRTRAVATA!

RAPHAEL (*the same as up to now, with no one doubting that he is doing anything more than translate Tanasîcu's previous shout*): "I ought to have broken your neck long ago. But I took pity and I didn't break it."

TANASÎCU: DIRDASIN STIR STRASC GUODAMOTO!

RAPHAEL (*translates*): "And it was much better that I didn't break it. What blame did poor neck of yours have? Just you carry on like this… And I'll crush your head instead! …"

WALDO (*not seeming to care about these threats one whit. He grins in satisfaction. He leans on his other elbow, thereby changing the direction of his attack. He now focuses his attention on his next prey*): And with what ailment were you saying you're worried I might be exceedingly ill, Marcel dear?

PICA (*instinctively seeking to avoid a confrontation*): What would the date today be? Why is it we have to put up with hunger today too?! Like yesterday, when they pulled our guts out and thrashed them with a stick. Hunger says that every day is a Thursday.

MARCEL (*well-meaning, to Waldo*): How do I know?! Maybe it's Thursday. I've pulled my fingers out of the little one's ears, Waldo, so that he won't start crying. Anything. Maybe you caught a draught and your ears are stuffed up. Or maybe you got it straight from that little one of yours.

Maybe he sneezes, coughs… (*Studying Waldo with the utmost seriousness, however*): But you don't look as though you're that ill…

WALDO (*with sweetness in his voice*): Thank you. But in your peaceful, restful moments, Marcel dear. Have you ever asked yourself. Why you haven't seen me. With that child of mine in my arms, which you're always mentioning?

MARCEL: Maybe you've sent him to summer camp… Or nursery. It's not healthy to get mixed up in other people's problems… In any case, you're a bad parent, you know, if you don't let him breastfeed.

WALDO: I'm continually breastfeeding him. Sometimes I bathe him… I don't neglect – not for my life – to dry him… To powder his little feet and his botty with talc. And, at the very end, I of course change his nappy.

MARCEL: You've got some sense back into your head.

WALDO: Sure. But you know what it would be called in medical terms if, for example, I were to perform all these wonderful things. I mean, if I were to bathe, swaddle and breastfeed the baby? Without there being any baby?

MARCEL: Parental love.

WALDO: Medical experts, Marcel… Wouldn't you rush off all at once to the medical experts if so much as a fingernail of that little one of yours fell ill?! …And wouldn't you listen with the blindest faith to every little word with which they might help you to overcome his illness?

MARCEL: I'd even have faith in you, if you could cure him for me! …But first of all, you'll have to convince me how correctly you breastfeed that little one of yours.

WALDO: It is a wise precaution. However, we all find ourselves under the omnipotence of medical experts. (*He settles himself more firmly on his rump. He changes the place of a few coverlets, to confuse his listeners. And, all of a sudden, he rummages in the innards of his mattress and extracts a huge psychiatry book.*) Behold! …The crème de la crème! …See how the gilt letters are arrayed and encrusted on a book in which all the cleverness in the world is laid up! (*He caresses the covers of the tome and wipes them with the unravelled fabric of his pyjamas.*) Four authors. Such as the world has never seen… The first is a university professor! …The second is also a university professor. The third is only a university doctor… And the last! …A more threatening rank has not even been invented in the scientific hierarchy: Academician! …

GEORGE (*unimpressed*): What's he called?

WALDO (*not condescending to answer*): A veritable molehill of medical specialists. Let us delight our minds… with what they have written (*he flicks through the pages*) on page… 314.

LUPU (*endeavouring to distract his attention*): Ooo-oo! …Ooo-oo!

WALDO: Scat!

LUPU: Has your pup hunted turtledoves or copious woodpecker eggs today, Marcel?

WALDO: I'll scald that scraggy back of yours, you numbskull! …Get over here. Prick up your ears, you mangy carnivore… Page 314. Starting at the second paragraph. (*He is obviously improvising, interweaving his personal inventions with phrases which are really taken from the dog-eared psychiatry tome*): "Hallucinations… hmm… hmm… hmm… Pathological precepts with no real object. The most repugnant, fatal, contagious illness in the world… The idiots who catch it hear in their mind, mistakenly: growling bears, jingling bells, and mewling cats…" (*To Marcel*): Which is to say, what you're suffering from.

MARCEL (*sincerely*): This looks like it's been written by the one who only got as far as university professor. It's obvious he had an antipathy towards studying. And whenever he could he used to go off to parties to escape from the other medical experts.

WALDO: No. In this illness we are reading about, he became an academician. The academician. His study on "the – most – deadly – illness – in – the – world" so enthused the examiners that, not having enough room on his examination paper to give him straight A's, they had to write their congratulations on each other's cheeks.

MARCEL: Maybe they were his brothers.

WALDO: Possibly. But it's very rare for an academician to have other academician brothers… Let's now listen to the essence of these medical experts' entire wisdom… The underlined portion. Paragraph number three (*he improvises in the same way as before*): "The hallucinations are to be encountered in cases of lesion of the occipital lobe… putrefaction, dementia, epilepsy… The most dangerous form of hallucination, however, is when the idiot, clutching a bunch of filthy rags to his breast… and thinking that this bunch of rags is his baby… breastfeeds, coddles, bathes, and administers medicaments to the bunch of rags… Then… the only remedy for this terrifying illness… is for a courageous man to approach the idiot on tiptoes and shoot his bunch of rags!"

MARCEL: Waldo, I'm very much afraid that your medical experts are sneaking into the summer camp right now and, if it's not well guarded, they're going to shoot your baby.

(*The entire ward, minus Marcel and Waldo, burst out laughing, in grunts and squeals. A first group is laughing because of the amusement produced by Marcel's riposte. A second group is merely affected by the agitation induced by the first.*
   Without betraying even the most fleeting emotion, Waldo elegantly closes his treatise. He affectionately wipes it with his sleeve. And he stows it, with infinite care, somewhere in the guts of his mattress.
   After the infernal din has died down, there are a few seconds of silence. Then…)

PICA: Can you tell me how many days of plaster meatballs have passed already?! …Because I'm really bloated… And the stomach of my left intestine is aching! …The poor blighter, isn't he allowed to eat at least some sawdust moussaka?

GEORGE (*before speaking, he removes from his mouth the handkerchief he permanently sucks, in order to quell the agonies provoked by a lack of alcohol. His eyes gleam. He is salivating because of the idea he has had. He speaks haughtily, with feigned indifference. He avoids making it obvious that he is laying a trap for Pica*): How the hell can I sell you any more sawdust if you don't squeeze a drop of medicinal spirit out of that cow *Olympia*?! …Here's how we'll do it… You hit yourself just once – but hard – against the iron edge of the bed… Blood gurgles up from your forehead… And then that stingy bitch, for fear of getting a fine, stuffs the crack with a great big wad of cotton wool… Oozing medicinal spirit! …You hand me the spirit, and I hand you all the grub.

PICA (*more than won over. But in order to convince himself one hundred per cent that George has understood*): An iron bed I have. Do you have some sawdust?

ZOLI (*bursts in, out of the blue, without any connexion to the discussion up to now. He speaks using only residual expressions that have attached themselves to his deficient psyche. He does not understand the meaning of any of the words he uses*): Where are we dying today? …Because if I die on a Tuesday. You should arrange to die on a Thursday…

THE PRINCE (*as though he were being accused of having caused it, he interrupts in order to disperse the effects of Zoli's macabre line*): Really! Gentlemen! What is the date today? …However many heroic trials we may be subjected to, it is really inappropriate for us to do so without even knowing what date it is…. Especially on the morning when we have brought to a conclusion the most significant of timber transactions!

MARCEL (*deep in thought for a few seconds. Then he is convinced*): It is 15 April 1645.

CAIUS: It's 105 April 200,004. Beat you! …Wasn't it you who said that the rules say we're playing for the highest number?!

LUPU: It might be twenty two-ooo! …(*He howls like a wolf.*) Twenty two-ooo! January… I feel cold.

RAPHAEL: I'm sorry. I don't think it's January.

WALDO: Kiss the soles of my feet with your ungrateful, toothless mouths! …And then maybe I'll tell you what date it is.

GEORGE: It's my cock's birthday.

ZOLI: It's 23 August, you cow! There's a parade. Tomorrow, keep close. You'll see how it rounds the bend by the food shops at great speed… And when they're not looking. Quick, jump on them! And they'll get to selling hens to the populace in droves…

PICA: If it doesn't come with sawdust moussaka, I'll throw up. And let him gobble up my hens at least.

GEORGE: It falls on my cock's birthday!

TANASÎCU: PRIX PRAX TANATVULGORUM DUCADILADIUS MALACSINO! …DUALCARPENTRY!

KIRILL (*out of the blue, interrupting as though he were translating for Tanasîcu*): If I die a little, wake me up!

RAPHAEL (*takes on a luminous, chastened appearance, translating, as usual, the sayings of Tanasîcu. Sayings which, this time, seems to have been understood by all, excepting Cirill*): "The date is precisely… 31 August, the holy feast.."

KIRILL (*again out of the blue, in conclusion to what he has said above*): Nip my pen and I shall be resurrected! …

RAPHAEL (*serenely passes over Kirill's interruption, going on to explain Tanasîcu's declaration*): "This year, 31 August has seemingly come upon us unawares… We have two or three more hours to wait. And towards afternoon, after midday, we shall slip. Once more. All of us. Gently. Into the Festival of Meetings!"

GEORGE (*staccato, inimically, nonetheless giving a very clear impression that he is addressing someone in particular*): It is very pleasant to me that we shall be slipping into the swindle you are talking about... Who is it you want to meet? As for me, the Festival will give me a chance to meet with your ma for a little...

PICA (back to front, illogically, just to show his disapproval of George's openly insulting intervention): I'm not selling you any more sawdust.

KIRILL (also talking nonsense, but with an animation that no one would have suspected): Listen to them! ...Listen to them! When they heard, the poor dear, the thump on the floor...

THE PRINCE (listening and then commencing to talk under the influence of a vision by which he is gradually overwhelmed): Yes, they set out... In the cellar beneath us their bodies jolted... They unfastened the handcuffs in which, shackled, they have been waiting for hundreds of years... Bolts of lightning go with them... The stone flags of this floor, as well as the cigarette papers, will melt! ...And, in the only visit they undertake once a year... In our ward. Ascending among us. Four consummate gentlemen will make their appearance...

MARCEL: No, not four. If we don't take into account the babies, at least six.

CAIUS: No, not six. Eight.

LUPU: No-oooo! However many they'll be wolves.

THE PRINCE (under the same vision): Four persons with a wholly flawless distinction. Servants of the four most important religions in the world! ... Who, during the course of a single day, will compete among themselves, expositing their teachings and seeking to attract adepts from among us, each for his own God... And if one alone from among them – a thing that has never happened before – succeeds in winning over to the religion he serves... absolutely all twelve of us who dwell here... Then the earth will quake! The walls will leap in terror like lambs... And the God for whom all twelve of our souls have been won... will descend to his servant!! ...

He will slay all the other three lying priests. He will lift his blessed servant up to Heaven... And us, his new adepts and saints, us he will release from here, curing all the illnesses that some among us might suffer! Endowing us with eternal life!! ...And granting us the favour of becoming rich princes!! ...Just as I am in any case a prince!

MARCEL (*unimpressed*): See, that's why my friend Pica's a more decent bloke... He pesters us only with his sawdust supplies. He doesn't do our heads in with the affliction... that we have to become princes.

GEORGE (*with apparent wisdom, as though he wished to reconcile them*): Know something? (*To the Prince*): Bugger your princes!

THE PRINCE: Listen to them! ...To them listen! ...Straighten your neckties, for now I set out!

CAIUS: You're not going to tell me that it's me who's all eight of them. Who ascend with their medicaments and their scimitars. And who indeed heal and cast to the ground everything in their path?!

THE PRINCE: Whoever doesn't have a tie, let his smooth him top hat! Whoever doesn't have a top hat, let him sell his sword to buy one. Because it is never appropriate to greet saviours without a top hat on.

ZOLI (*jumping to his feet from the bed in which he has been lying stock-still, bursts into a song whose words, although he himself does not understand their import, spread horror among the other patients*):

> There was an auntie blonde
> who fell into the pond! ...
>
> She went to bite some flies
> and what she bit was eyes! ...
>
> And when she went to mow
> with a sickle she did go! ...

She shot the cake in the head
and now the cake lies dead…

KIRILL (from this moment, he starts to talk with two voices, proof that another person, from another, diabolical realm has installed himself inside his body, possessing him. The voices, which speak alternately, are dramatically different. Sometimes the voices quarrel among themselves, as now):

--VOICE NUMBER 1 (the demented voice with which Kirill has spoken up to now): You're here again? …He's here again… He won't even wait for the paint to dry on my bodywork. Because he comes. To mount me. And he tells me I'm his motorcycle… But why don't you go inside someone else?

--VOICE NUMBER 2 (a terrifying, croaking voice of demonic possession, seemingly emerging from his bowels, but demonstrating a wholly different kind of thought: limpid, flawless, coherent, but at the same time cunning and unexpectedly destructive): Leave it out, you'll be gnawing your fingers when I bring another few cousins to live in your… What's all this stinking filth you're greeting me with inside? Didn't I order you to clean up in here?

--VOICE NUMBER 1: What do you think I am? …A hotel? …Clean it up yourself! …I'm going to kick your motorcycle to pieces.

--VOICE NUMBER 2 (ignoring Voice Number 1 for a time, and addressing the other patients): Make that devil *Zoli* sing a bit more quietly. So that he won't spoil the Festival and bring us bad luck.

MARCEL (with conviction. And, as usual, without a trace of mockery): If he doesn't make the table fly up to the ceiling for me like a sparrow. And make the lamps tell us all kinds of amusing stories, so that they'll even almost make the little one laugh… *Virgil* was right: they can sit on their bottoms or on their heads, I still won't believe in them!

WALDO: This year, not even a minute of the Festival of Meetings is going to take place!

KIRILL (with VOICE NUMBER 2, with which he sweetens or mangles words, depending on the case, suiting it to the voice of his interlocutor, in order to gain a greater influence over the other patients. Now, he pretends to pick up on a hidden meaning to Waldo's words, which he approves of and develops): Yes. And when it's not fully going to take place…

WALDO (*with hypocritical amazement. He understands in an instant the bewildering slyness and servility present in VOICE NUMBER 2, Kirill's devil voice. He is enthused by the new turn in the discussion. He throws himself into the game*): Well! And what are we going to do to the four of them?! …When we wait for them by the hole in the floor through which they will make their appearance in the ward. Shall we bid them welcome? Shall we ask after their health? …Are we going to butcher them?! …

VIRGIL (*still apathetic, with bloodshot eyes, not understanding the plot that is being hatched*): No. But if they don't let us go home to this Festival either…

GEORGE: When the priests will be chanting and preaching, in full flow, with all that shit. And from their liturgies. We'll sneak up on their arses… Each holding a plank… Or one of the lead pipes from the beds…

VIRGIL (*still profoundly disoriented. He lifts his head. And, as though asleep, he nonetheless enters the groove of the other three conspirators' plotting*): No. But if somehow they forbid us to leave here again, to go home… And we'll crack open their skulls… Like eggshells, placed in huge baskets of eggs…

PICA (*vociferating from his place, on his favourite subject. But what he babbles has no connexion to the plan of aggression, which the conspirators are weighing up a few feet away*): It's pointless him promising me… sausages with whipped cream, religion in the other world… If he can't give me, in my mouth, to munch, at least two handfuls of iron filings, right now!

KIRILL (*with VOICE NUMBER 2*): …And we'll teach them what they were commanded and what is forbidden. The other suckers. We'll preach to them, from their religions…

GEORGE (*surprised. He takes his handkerchief out of his mouth. He speaks. He thrusts the handkerchief back*): What's your religion?

KIRILL (*with VOICE NUMBER 2*): The one with… The one which talks about…

WALDO (*looks ironically at Kirill. Addressing Kirill, George and Virgil*): Leave it. We'll sort out the religious doctrines at the right time. In the second phase.

GEORGE (*the handkerchief. Taking up the thread of the plot*): …We'll dress up in their clobber. And we'll sell… (*points at the rest of the patients*) to these idiots the miracles and tricks we steal from the priests. But that… errr … that only after… errr… (*For a while he can no longer speak, because of strong salivation produced by pleasure.*) Their relatives will buy, from us, for them, cures. Paying us in bottles and demijohns gushing alcohol! …

KIRILL (*with VOICE NUMBER 2, with servility, seeking to rectify his previous hesitation*): …Only after all of them kiss the soles of Waldo's feet… as he commanded them to five minutes ago… "with their ungrateful, toothless mouths"! …

(*The group of conspirators pause in their enthusiasm for a moment. Waldo, George and Kirill look amicably, encouragingly or impatiently, waiting, each in his own way, to see the reaction of the weak link in their chain. The attention of all three is focussed on Virgil. At last*):

VIRGIL (*his eyes almost bulging out of their sockets. Sweating. Prey to an uncontrollable inner turmoil*): And… err… Only after they bring their… wives. And their sisters here to us. So that… so that…

(*After three seconds, Waldo, brimming with generosity, makes a gesture of imperial benevolence with one finger, thereby urging that Virgil be assisted*):

GEORGE (*benevolently*): So that we can drink their flacons of perfume and stick our cocks in them!

END OF ACT ONE

ACT TWO

THE SET

The same masterpiece of universal psychiatric ward scenery. The same twelve patients as in the first act.

In the second act, the light is more intense, accompanying at a visual level the arrival of the four religious representatives in the ward. The room is cleaner, the maelstroms of filth attenuated.

On stage, the Festival of Meetings has begun.

Having emerged, from the cellars of the psychiatric ward, the four religious teachers – Paranasius (the Orthodox priest), Igantius (the Roman-Catholic priest), Amanda (the Buddhist monk), and Zaid (the Muslim imam) – are new human presences in the ward. Given that it is the Festival of Meetings, their aim is to meet the patients, preach to them, and attempt to convert – each to his own religion – the twelve patients.

These four religious leaders sit at a long table with their backs to the window and facing the twelve inmates.

In the middle of the table stands a wooden cube, encasing a clock on each side. The size of the clocks is that of a large alarm clock, with a diameter of 4-6 inches.

These four clocks can be started or stopped by pressing a button at the top, one for each timepiece. By means of the four clocks, the four leaders can in turn measure their preaching time, during which they will exposit the main teachings of the religions they represent. The duration of the preaching time for each of the four is equal.

The religious leader whose turn has come to preach rises from the long table, sits in the middle of the room (on a chair or on a rug, according to preference), and from there seeks to instruct and convert the twelve patients.

After his preaching time has expired, each religious leader returns to his place at the table alongside the other three religious guides.

The second act of the play opens at the moment in which the Buddhist monk, Amanda, glowing with serenity and inner harmony, is nearing the end of his sermon.

AMANDA: Let me recapitulate for you all... (*A moment of silence and concentration on what is about to be said*): So, seven years after abandoning all his palaces and riches, as well as his two wives... As he was sitting plunged in meditation, at the root of a tree...

KIRILL (*with VOICE NUMBER 2, extremely obligingly*): What sort of tree?

AMANDA: A fig tree.

MARCEL (*benevolently*): Aha!

LUPU (*neutrally*): As soon as you start teaching fig trees history, you come up against the most stubborn creatures in the world!

AMANDA (*invulnerable to interruptions; he continues to exposit his teaching with the same calm and with the same near perfect harmony*): As he was sitting, deep in thought, at the root of a tree. One night. Unexpectedly. All of a sudden... The truth powerfully shone within his mind!

THE PRINCE: He was a king. So, he wasn't wearing specs and a beret... He was a crowned head. So, he wouldn't have permitted himself to pick pockets... How then could the truth not have shone within his mind, and with so much power?!

GEORGE (*he pulls the handkerchief out of his mouth, solely to repeat mockingly what Amanda has previously stated*): In other words, he stopped hiccupping. His eyes were popping out from the concentration. And he asked himself: What the blazes am I doing here?

IGNATIUS (*at the table, he is seated closest to the apparatus made up of four embedded clocks, of which only that of the Buddhist speaker is measuring time. Due to the frequent interruptions of the patients, Ignatius makes a gesture as though to stop the clock. Concomitantly, he addresses Amanda*): Shall I interrupt your preaching time, reverend Amanda?

PICA: If he didn't look after his guts properly, it was pointless him pretending to have been brought up in palaces! ...

AMANDA: The truth then shone powerfully within his mind. He discovered that the whole of existence is suffering... That release from suffering comes about only through suppression of the desire to live... From the moment of this discovery, he was no longer Prince Siddhartha, the one who had fled from his palaces, but rather he became, as those around him also named him: the Enlightened or Buddha. The Buddha revealed to his disciples the four holy truths: the existence of suffering, the cause of suffering, the removal of suffering... and the way that leads to the removal of suffering.

CAIUS (*he has desperately been seeking to understand something from the learning exposited by Amanda. He has not succeeded and even now he understands absolutely nothing. When he hears "the four holy truths" being enumerated, Caius strives to memorise them, counting them on the fingers of his left hand. But he cannot follow Amanda, gets mixed up, and is left looking ridiculous and revolted, with his fingers spread out in the air*): This is a way for just one hand... You see how you're resorting to trickery?! Didn't you yourself say that there were, errr... some sixteen or seventeen ways?

AMANDA: No. I never pronounced such a thing. I merely stated that the fourth truth, the holy way. The way that leads to the removal of suffering. Separates, in its turn, into eight paths. The eight paths are: right belief, right decision, right speaking, right deeds, right means of existence, right effort, right thinking and right meditation.

PICA: Those girls, if they drove away the prince... Maybe they used to feed even his guts with right injection, holy tablet, noble electric shock. Thirty-seven – fifty-one ways... Poor Marcel is right.

MARCEL: Me, as for being poor, I wouldn't be that poor. I've got a child. Maybe you haven't got... That brick you gnaw, you think that it's a child?

PICA: The brick is a little boy. I have a little piece of slate too. Two. A little boy and a little girl.

MARCEL: You've ended up a cannibal. There is no greater villainy to which bad friendships can impel you! The cannibals you've ganged up with – precisely because they're cannibals – are going to be hanged along whatever path they take! (*To Amanda, with sympathy*): Isn't that right, baldy?

IGNATIUS (*to the same Amanda*): You have one minute remaining for your sermon, your honour. I have stopped the clock.

WALDO (*to Ignatius, dryly*): I told you not to stop it and you've stopped it. You did a bad thing when you stopped it, given that I asked you not to stop it, your holiness... (*Striving to conceal his fury, he resorts to a smile.*) Why should we drag it out?

VIRGIL: It is a sin to play with the clock.

WALDO (*turning back to Amanda, in order to hurry him into continuing and make him finish his sermon*): So, all is suffering. Four holy ways. The fourth way has eight paths... Please jump straight to the part with nirvana, the bit with the smoke, and let's conclude.

AMANDA (*undisturbed, without irony*): Do you wish to listen to nirvana for one minute or for two minutes?

WALDO: You are a very diplomatic chap. You choose.

AMANDA: The whole of reality is an illusion. Try to clutch between your fingers any of life's promises and you will find only smoke... People die, people are reincarnated, people endlessly suffer once more. In order to interrupt the entire chain of reincarnations and of suffering, the first three things that must be abandoned are: the thirst for life, attachment to the world, and ignorance of the truth that would halt rebirth... He who has been enlightened that all is illusion and who has single-handedly broken the shackles of his reincarnations, who has elevated himself to the state of bodhi and penetrated into nirvana. Nirvana means extinguishing. Emancipation from pain. Nothingness. Annihilation...

GEORGE (*the handkerchief*): So I'm more dangerous if I say not "go to blazes" but "go to nirvana".

MARCEL (*to Pica in particular*): And whatever path you take with the cannibals, you end up either hanged or annihilated...

WALDO (*calm, tactful, he is sitting upright in bed, like the majority of the patients, with his back resting against a pillow. He is going by his own stopwatch, which he has long since extracted from inside the mattress, and he makes it understood that this is the primary instrument for measuring the preaching times of the four religious teachers. The apparatus consisting of the four clocks, as in a chess match, enthroned on the table, would have no other purpose than that of not deviating however little from the time measured by his, Waldo's, stopwatch*): Fifteen seconds. Thirteen... Eight... Five. Three. Two. Stop! (*To Amanda*): And the second allotted time for preaching, that of your reverend self, has come to a close. (*Addressing them all*): The Orthodox did more ranting than he did preaching. The Buddhist has initiated us. But in my eyes, I still don't feel as though the little lights that ought to have been kindled in the eyes of any believer or adept have lit up. (*He turns and talks familiarly with the Orthodox priest, an old man with a huge white beard and a venerable appearance*): Isn't that so, Bowel of Hell?

(*During this time, Amanda, in silence, has risen from the place where he exposited his teaching and sat down at the table where the other three high religious servants are lined up. In this way, the order in which the four religious leaders are seated on the bench is as follows: Paranasius, Amanda – both of them having completed their times for preaching – Ignatius – who is about to speak – and Zaid*).

PARANASIUS (*being the one aimed at by Waldo's question, answers him, with a resounding voice well-trained in oratory*): May the worms devour you, father! They have not been kindled for you.

WALDO (*politely, as though he were responding to a greeting*): May the heavens strike you down, father! I would have scratched myself had I felt... (*Sweetly, as though the question had nothing to do with the main thread of the discussions*): What is it that you are taught in the holy Psalter to recommend to those who swear by things holy?

PARANASIUS (*it is plain that he is straining his memory and that he is quoting from the Homilies*): "For the blasphemer, the canon that is laid down is for him to drag his tongue along the ground many times. Let him be taught wisdom by beatings... And if need be, break his teeth, rend his mouth. Sanctify thy hand with such a blow..."

WALDO: A terrifying canon! Well then, you shouldn't swear...

PARANASIUS (*humanly disconcerted that precisely he is being instructed to avoid such a blasphemous act*): Me, swear?!

WALDO: We know that, as a rule, you speak only like an innocent little bird...

GEORGE (*takes out his handkerchief, giving what has been said an obscene signification*): Yes. Like a little bird.

WALDO: But if I were to tell you that…

(*And here, for a few moments, Waldo ceases to speak. Giving a heavy hint, he looks at the three plotters who belong to his group. He thereby warns them that he is about to utter the first keyword, which all four of them have agreed upon shortly beforehand. The first keyword, known only to the four plotters, as well as to the readers of this director's edition of the play, is the word "beard".*

Indeed, when they hear the first keyword, the word "beard", uttered by Waldo, the other three, George, Virgil and Kirill will rise from the strategic points where they have been lying in wait and, mingling with the other two patients who are walking randomly around the ward, Lupu and the Prince, they will approach, as though by accident, the bed of Zoli, the oligophrenic patient, who will continue to look at them inertly.

They will move Zoli to one side. They will lift up his mattress. And from the frame of Zoli's bed, the three – George, Virgil and Kirill – will arm themselves with three huge metal bars, which they will endeavour to conceal beneath their ragged pyjama tops.

Due to his inductive or imitative behaviour, Caius will join the three. And, although he has not previously plotted with any of them, Caius too will receive an iron bar, becoming inveigled into many of the subsequent scuffles, carried along by the wave, without premeditation.

Meanwhile, Waldo resumes the discussion, seeking to hold the attention of the rest of the audience on an entirely different object than his little army arming themselves with iron clubs.)

WALDO: But if I were to tell you: "What a lice-ridden highwayman's beard you have! ...Not to mention the fact that it's pathetically short... Given that it's not even long enough for you to wipe your bottom with it!" ...Well, could you, your holiness, make any reply to that?

PARANASIUS (*with dignity*): I could answer: "May the winds from the devils' backsides blow away the dandelion fluff off your chest!" ...But also: "May the gristles of your heart be cast to the four winds, anathematised wretch. May your scattered bones never be put back together!"

WALDO (*with delight*): A holy man!

PARANASIUS (*seriously*): Or I might also say to you that: "May your guts be coiled round the baptismal font, and let the devil, poor wretch, fornicate with your mother in it!" ... But...

WALDO: We know. You are not allowed to. So it was better that you did not say... (*And as proof of the fact that he has learned almost by heart the interdiction which, it is to be supposed, was, in the past, drummed into the head of Paranasius, he recites*): "There is a way of speaking and a way of saying..."

PARANASIUS (*adding the rest*): "... which work hand in hand..."

WALDO (*finishing it off*): "... and with death alike."

PARANASIUS: Truly do they work, father! From the treasury of all goodness they do separate you. And onto your knees they do throw you... Taking the Lord's name in vain... they drive you to hearken and to bow to the Unclean One! ...

MARCEL (*meditatively*): Aha.

GEORGE (*not because he has garnered any additional grudge against*

Paranasius, but he cannot control himself): Go to the Devil!

WALDO (*ironically, to George*): As for you, you would have permission to speak. But don't do it. It doesn't sit well... (*Once again, to George, Virgil, Kirill, and even Caius*): As you were taught, regarding hygiene and the removal of dirt, in the writings of Saint... Porcius of Pie. (*The name is just as much a mockery as the quotation which is to follow...*)

(*At this moment, Waldo once more stops talking, and gives his unseen listeners the impression that he is improvising. As though he were undecided, he goes on to select absolutely at random an object in the ward and then passes it on to his acolytes, so that they can remove the dirt from it. Appearances make this deceptive method of understanding easier. George, Virgil, Kirill and Caius are even clutching a kind of rag for dusting.*

In reality, Waldo has paved the way for the enunciation of the second keyword of the plot, the word "window". At the moment they hear this second keyword launched, those in the commando of plotters separate in two: Kirill slinks to somewhere behind the beds lined up along the wall on the left of the stage. He leans against the wall and waits, unheeded by any of those present. George and Virgil, accompanied by Caius, silently slip over to the narrow gap between the window – barred with a thick wire mesh – and the table where the four religious servants are seated. The four religious representatives continue to look in the same direction as up to now, namely at Waldo and the majority of the patients, who have remained sprawled on their beds. And so, by a skilled flanking manoeuvre, George, Waldo and Caius are now stationed directly above the crowns of Paranasius', Amanda's, Ignatius' and Zaid's heads, and are capable at any moment of summarily smashing these crowns. They merely have to guess, from the play of Waldo's future words, which of the skulls of the four religious leaders they must crack open first.)

WALDO: "... Those of you who have not vouchsafed to cleanse even your own hearts, quick march and at least clean... the window..." And not to mention the fact that those who keep nagging you to cleanse your hearts ought first of all to be sure their own are clean! ... Did they or did they not keep the window clean?! ... Let us see... (*He inclines his torso forward slightly and addresses Paranasius alone.*) Is this not what the great theologian, Porcius of Pie, teaches us?! ...That once you have received your punishment, it means you already consider yourself guilty… Because as punishment, you've taken for yourself a missus priest, isn't that right, Underbelly of Hell?!

PARANASIUS: I had to, father. For ordination. To cook, sew, and clean around the house.

WALDO: …Nevertheless, having taken her, passionately and of your own will, you ought not to have driven her to an early grave, constantly clouting her across the mouth with the back of that pious hand of yours. And when you didn't finish her with the back of your pious hand, father, you used a bunch of twigs to beat her over the head… Well, won't you have angered Saint Porcius by these deeds?!

(*At the moment Waldo begins speaking to him, George, Virgil and Caius mass above the skull of Paranasius. The three are carefully weighing every word uttered. They seek to gauge exactly how irritated or well-disposed Waldo is. From time to time, they wave their iron bars over Paranasius' head, ready at any time to take the life of the Orthodox priest.*)

PARANASIUS: Before I married her, son, she used to hold her tongue, and she looked as comely as an icon. But not one single day had elapsed since the wedding when I found that she had begun, out of the blue, to curse at me with putrid words – swearing by God, by the Holy Virgin, by Christ, by the Cross – whenever she saw me! …I was horrified… But not much time passed before I noticed that whenever my lady wife opened her lips to spew her blasphemous words – bang! – a huge serpent would thrust out its head… it would dangle there… it would dangle and then slither back inside my wife's mouth… Now, my greatest fear was that it might descend from there and make its nest among the furniture of my home.

WALDO: And so how did you proceed, your holiness?

PARANASIUS: With many tears I begged her to abandon her beastly way of life… But when I sensed that my holy counsel was not taking effect quickly enough, I would daze her with the stick! …

WALDO: Stern priest! (*With a broad smile, he dissipates the tense atmosphere that had been growing as regards the fate of Paranasius' life.*) I don't think that even St Porcius could have been more profoundly moved by such pious perseverance! (*In the next sentence he tries to imitate Paranasius' manner of talking.*) "Wielding the wood, I managed to deliver the poor woman from the whirlwind of sins…" (*He resumes his usual tone of voice and addresses the same Paranasius.*) Ultimately, not even the Patriarchate ordained you so that you could be a snake keeper in the zoo… And so, you see, as far as you are concerned, the word "window" does not yet apply.

(*From the place where they have been watching, namely above the head of Paranasius, the three, George, Virgil and Caius, relax. They grimace. And, for the moment, they conceal the iron bars they have been waving over the skull of the Orthodox priest.*)

The four religious representatives are not, and nor will they become, aware of the danger that literally hovers over their heads.

WALDO (*ceremoniously, to Paranasius*): Your holiness, wise Paranasius, sit to the right of his enlightenment Amanda! …And let us now find out why St Porcius is angry with him…

(*The three, George, Virgil, and Caius, taking their iron bars with them, move one step to the left, setting up "camp" above the head of Amanda.*)

AMANDA (*with his usual serenity*): I am not an enlightenment, but merely a humble Buddhist monk, whose name, in this existence, is Amanda. But if you want to call me "your enlightenment", call me "your enlightenment". If you do not want to call me it, do not call me it.

(*The three proceed, highly delighted, to wave their iron bars. They make disparaging signs to each other regarding the Buddhist monk's chances of survival. Silently and mockingly, they imitate the movements of Amanda's mouth.*)

WALDO (*addressing Amanda*): Are you Buddhists not the wise believers who claim that, in order to liberate yourselves from suffering, you must not worship God?! In fact, you cannot even see any reason why you should recognise that God exists…?!

PICA (this time he proves to be the meditative one): Aha!

AMANDA (sorely trying the patience of many of them with his patience):
Neither do we say that God does not exist. Nor do we say that God exists.
All we say is that, in order to liberate ourselves, it is not necessary for us to
take into account such a hypothesis.

WALDO: Nicely put! But, you see, it's a widespread hypothesis… Let's
suppose that St Porcius would not be angry at the stupidities you claim…
That in his magnanimity, he would judge you only according to the way
in which you fulfil certain things, things you yourselves demand in your
teaching.

*MARCEL (well-meaning, desirous to help Amanda, he anticipates the way in
which he thinks the practising Buddhist is going to answer)*: "Neither do I say
let me be judged. Nor do I say let me not be judged…"

*ZOLI (interrupting, as usual without rhyme or reason, without any connexion
to the twists and turns of the discussion. He seems to be addressing Amanda
in particular)*: From the way you're scratching your ear so guiltily, it's
Thursday.

WALDO (to Amanda): So, are you not the ones who warn that first among
the virtues of those who pursue perfection is not to kill absolutely any
living thing, however insignificant?!

*AMANDA (calmly takes from his girdle, which is below the level of the table
top and thus masked, a certain object, which he raises to show them all)*: This is
the sieve through which, since I was admitted among the monks, I have
daily strained water, so as not to swallow heedlessly any mite or fly…
Moreover, in the lands whence I come, during the entire rainy season, it
was forbidden for us to leave the precincts of the monastery, so as not to
crush, unawares, even a single beetle under our heel in the tall grass.

LUPU (with aplomb and an unjustifiable hatred): Orientals aren't beetles.
They're daisies.

THE PRINCE (*looking attentively towards the empty space by the sink, as though he were seriously evaluating certain lofty objects which might still be displayed there*): Some precious stones, those I gave as gifts this morning to some natives who travelled through this room, seem to be missing.

WALDO (*to Amanda*): The whole charm of your personality is that you abide by the interdictions. You don't try to pass over the rainy season in silence. But, not even for your life, will you admit that you murdered the little beetle… But some fifty years ago, weren't you the one, your holiness, who was galloping in pursuit of an amorous Buddhist nun, from Sri Lanka, with a mind to roll on the ground with her, over the fields, and who, on that occasion, squashed more than a cartload brimful of beetles?!!!…

AMANDA (*with the same inner harmony, immovable in what he upholds, patiently*): It is true that fifty years ago. But it is not true that in the rainy season… It is true that in Sri Lanka. But it is not true that over the fields… It is true that, under the guidance of a guru, I experimented, together with a novice, with a series of tantric procedures, of psychical immersions in the impure, exercising esoteric sensuality. Black magic. Idolatrous belief. And wilful immorality. But it is not true that I killed, be it even on that occasion, so much as a single insect. All the procedures in question I executed only in my mind.

MARCEL: What do you mean?! When you were prancing and whinnying after a lady Buddhist? When you were tearing off the little sparrow's clothes, with your teeth, only in your mind?

AMANDA: Perfectly true.

WALDO (*with humour*): To the devil with the hypothesis you won't take into account if you say it's perfectly true! (*He smiles broadly at Amanda, brimming with hypocritical magnanimity, the same as he had smiled at Paranasius a little earlier*). In the end, compared with the terrifying depravations condemned in the sacred writings of Porcius, the whopping lie becomes almost a good deed… And the window of the soul of your holiness seems reasonably well cleaned! …

(*Noticing the goodwill accorded to Amanda by Waldo, the three attackers, George, Virgil and Caius, once more relax. They grin with the same ferocity as they had smiled before. Again they secrete their iron bars in the questionable hiding place of their pyjama tops.*)

WALDO: In the end, when it saw you engaging in sexual immorality in your minds, what was the beetle doing when it crawled under the novice's bottom?!

LUPU (*pigmenting his words, as well as the other segments of time in which he merely crawls around agitatedly on all fours and takes no part whatsoever in the discussions, with lupine howls*): Since the emergence – owooo! – of the canonical writings, as well as the Dhammapada, through its lofty precepts Buddhism has sought to heal a part of the wounds of the oriental peoples... By proclamation of non-violence it identified a number of the places of these wounds. By abolition of the horri --- owooo! – ble system of separating men into castes it laved those wounds with water. But when it comes to disinfecting and dressing them, what does it – owooo! – what does it care?! ...

WALDO (*with a cordiality that indicates precisely the absolute lack of importance he accords to Lupu*): Scat! (*He kicks him.*)

(*Lupu yelps and hides under the bed.*)

WALDO (*ceremoniously, to Amanda*): So, please be seated also, your enlightenment... exactly in the place where you are sitting! ...Concentrate. Breathe, just as you know how, in a certain rhythm only. Whatever happens, close the gates of your soul to the outside world...

(*The three, George, Virgil and Caius, slap Amanda – in mockery, but also in a certain sort of friendliness – on the shoulders, then on his shaven pate. They arouse no suspicion in the other three religious representatives, who are still sitting at the table.*)

MARCEL: Why should he close them! 'Cause for the past half hour, as long as I've been watching him, he hasn't stopped gnawing at the suspenders of that gobby Buddhist nun…

PICA: In his mind?

MARCEL: How should I know?! … Only in his mind, I think.

THE PRINCE: All the more so, the rules of chivalry teach us that those dishonourable things which sometimes happen only in the mind, let's not even take them into account!

LUPU (very preoccupied and attentive, from under the bed): I think I… I can even hear her squealing. It makes my hackles rise whenever a Buddhist nun meets a Buddhist monk!

(Waldo has remained silent and, during the interval of time in which the turn of Marcel, Pica, the Prince, and Lupu has come to make a little conversation, he has shifted his entire attention from Amanda to the next religious leader in the order of those sitting on the bench. Waldo begins to gaze at Ignatius, the Roman-Catholic priest, sternly, in silence, fixedly and with an exceedingly evil eye, so that, in their varying degrees of understanding, his vengeful gaze, boding very great misfortune, escapes none of those in the ward. In any case, George, Virgil and Caius alter their facial expressions from mockery. They take the usual step to the left, shifting from above Amanda's pate to above Ignatius' skull. And they compose funereal faces for themselves.

The tension, having become exceedingly threatening, puts an end to the conversations. But, even at the moment when the tension will indeed reach the limit of the bearable, the one who will break the silence is precisely the one the others were least expecting.)

IGNATIUS (interrupts wholly unconcernedly, as though nothing bad was going to happen to him. He is cloying and speaks with an air of being the most agreeable and convincing man in the world. Like the other three religious leaders, he addresses himself to the patients in particular): My friends have very well remarked that, although Waldo has forbidden me to, it is only concern for their souls that has forced me to interrupt at this time… I did not wish to touch upon it, but I do touch upon it because I must reveal to you the ugly nature of this Buddhist false prophet! …

MARCEL (*stopping the "ears" of his rag baby, so that his "offspring" won't hear the words he is about to exclaim admiringly*): He's clever, the pig!

LUPU (*backing him up and augmenting his admiration*): He's a wolf!

(*On the other hand, Waldo and his group of conspirators are not at all impressed by Igantius' verbal performance. They remain silent and continue to cast the same looks of very ill omen.*)

IGNATIUS (*seeming to speak in a way that is completely relaxed and lacks even the slightest trace of concern. In reality, however, he has sharply sensed and understood the danger. From this moment, his entire efforts will concentrate only on maintaining the following balancing act: on the one hand, not to betray, however little, the terror that overwhelms him; on the other, to mollify the aggressive mood of the patients, however many concessions in terms of theology, or even enunciation of the worst heresies, it will cost him*): Even though last year many of you were irritated by the mystery of the Holy Trinity, it gladdened me… (*He quotes from memory*): "The Father is God. The Son is God. The Holy Spirit is God. But there are not three gods. But only a single God…" It's true, how can one understand such nonsense?! I confess that neither I understand anything about the Holy Trinity, nor the others who pretend to, not even as much as the dirt under your fingernails…

(*Waldo and those in his commando do not react positively to what they hear. They remain silent and merely look at Ignatius all the more terrifyingly.*)

THE PRINCE (*as though feeling the need to help Ignatius*): If we have made a gentlemen's agreement that it is a mystery, then mystery it is!

IGNATIUS (*continuing to raise the stakes, in order to defuse, by any means, the increasingly hostile atmosphere in the ward*): This wouldn't be the great mystery, the poor "Holy Trinity", but rather the fact that, although regarded as fundamental to the Roman-Catholic faith, God was nevertheless unimpressed and did not plan for the Trinity to be mentioned in so much as a single place in the Bible. (*Comically and affably, he raises his arms laterally in helplessness.*) It doesn't appear at all… (*He resumes his customary, serious tone.*) And so, your irritation, regarding the Holy Trinity,

I find perfectly justified…

PICA: The emperor's daughters must have given you some trick Bible.

MARCEL: The "Holy Trinity" mustn't have wanted you to read about it. 'Cause you're too ugly…

(Waldo is seemingly fit to burst from vexation.)

IGNATIUS (throws his final weapons into the fight): …What is more… The theological developments of the last few centuries run along exactly the same lines as your doubts about the Holy Trinity… *(He accentuates his tone of a lecturer concerned, above all, to win the assent of his listeners.)* The introduction of the dogmas regarding the "immaculate birth" – from her earthly parents Joachim and Ana – even in the case of Mary, the mother of Jesus. As well as that of the Ascension to Heaven of the body of the Virgin Mary have continuously strengthened the cult of her most often invoked as the "Mother of God"… *(With the utmost determination and emotion.)* And so – as you will agree – it won't be long before, instead of wasting our time praying to the Holy Trinity… we'll be praying directly to the "Holy Quaternity"! And you, as initiators of the newly revealed doctrine should be honoured as theologians! …

MARCEL (slightly disappointed, in a low voice, to Lupu): Some theologian you'd make! Saint Lupus!

WALDO (after the elapse of a pause for effect, unseals his dry lips, looks at Ignatius, as though he were seeing him for the first time, and asks him in a tone that is firm and, seemingly, for reasons known only to himself, overwhelmed by profound astonishment): … Do you know what St Porcius says about you?! …

(Subsequent events succeed each other at a rapid pace. Intuiting that George, Virgil and Caius, who have already raised their iron bars, will this time strike, Tanasîcu lets out a furious war cry.

The aphasic leader of the ward, massive and imposing, leaps from his bed and with a ferocious movement, he prepares to rush at the throats of those who are leisurely preparing to execute Ignatius.)

TANASÎCU (*giving his roar of a man pushed to the limit of endurance*): ARHANT ARHAVATA!

RAPHAEL (*"translates" his friends howl of rage almost concomitantly, but does not manage to carry the "translation" to its conclusion because of what happens to Tanasîcu*): "Don't you even think about touching…"

(*Kirill is the one who has stood apart from the rest of the group of conspirators, waiting without any to-do and almost unobserved, leaning against the wall opposite the one with the windows, and camouflaged behind the iron beds. A few dozen seconds before the moment in question, Kirill approached the head of Tanasîcu's bed.*

At the moment Tanasîcu releases his cry, leaps over the bed and rushes at George, Virgil and Caius, Kirill slips snake-like behind him and, with a terrible blow of the iron bar, he swinges the aphasic on the head.

Tanasîcu remains frozen for a second. Kirill immediately "has mercy" on him with a second blow, just as terrible, and then, using his shoulder and arms, pushes the falling body of Tanasîcu, causing it to topple, this time inert, crosswise onto the very bed from which, a short time before, it had leapt.

Kirill checks Tanasîcu's pulse. He grins. He has done a good job. Tanasîcu appears to be dead!

Kirill pulls the arms and legs of Tanasîcu's corpse, until he arranges him in the comfortable position in which he had been sitting a minute before, namely with his torso raised and leaning against the headboard of the bed and a pillow, and with his fingers interlocked above the blanket in which he is once more wrapped.)

KIRILL (*with VOICE NUMBER 2, applying the first blow of the iron bar to Tanasîcu's skull*): No it's not ARHANT ARHAVATA! (*And as he is performing the rest of the actions enumerated above, killing Tanasîcu and then manhandling his corpse*): More like… RANTA CANNAHAVA! …Meaning: "I, stupid Tanasîcu, am guilty! Like a humble servant I didn't implore him in time… in time… And those valiant lads had already got to thinking about touching him…"

(*After he has finished manhandling Tanasîcu's cadaver, sitting it up in bed, leaning it against the pillow, as though it were alive, Kirill suddenly whips out a highly whetted knife blade from under his pyjamas. And with this knife, wielding it just as swiftly and agilely, Kirill slits Tanasîcu's throat, from below the right ear all the way to below the left. From the still warm body of Tanasîcu a geyser of blood spurts from the seam of his slashed throat, splattering Kirill's pyjamas, Tanasîcu's blanket, George's empty bed alongside, and the floor.)*

KIRILL *(bellowing with VOICE NUMBER 2, his demonically possessed voice. He bellows with the voice of a demon as he cuts Tanasîcu's throat with the knife)*: I swore that I would suffocate you in your own blood! … I've finished you …It made me sick just looking at you, you decrepit old frying pan…

(Because of the cruelty and inhuman swiftness of Kirill, every single soul in the ward remains petrified. The only one who takes the risk of opposing the killer – not physically, it is true, but merely verbally – is Raphael, Tanasîcu's friend.)

RAPHAEL *(he flushes and makes his reedy and determined voice heard. He is in tears)*: Tanasîcu was not – he was never a decrepit old frying pan!

(Kirill twists around towards Raphael for an instant, but his features reveal how much he would despise himself were he, at this very moment, to waste his time crushing such an insignificant creature.
Kirill approaches the table. He lays the palms of his hands on the tabletop, planting himself face to face with George, Virgil and Caius, as well as the four religious leaders.)

KIRILL *(with VOICE NUMBER 2, addressing first of all to George, Virgil and Caius a question which he utters in the tone of a chat between friends)*: Well? … *(Then he lowers his eyes until they are boring into those of Ignatius. He asks him, very calmly, with friendliness and an unexpected and boundless pity)*: Haven't you found out what St Porcius has been saying about you?!

(Ignatius remains dumb. He is plunged into a superhuman terror.)

GEORGE *(in reply to the question Kirill has put to Ignatius, spits out his saliva-soaked handkerchief, and deftly wraps it around the Catholic priest's throat. And he explains to him)*: He says you're going to die!

(*With the same determination, George continues the operation. He quickly rolls the handkerchief from Ignatius' Adam's apple towards his nape, then vigorously grasps the ends in his fists and begins to throttle the Catholic priest with all his might. Ignatius' throat rattles. Then it no longer even rattles. He turns red. Then, losing consciousness, he turns purple. Were it not dangling in the harness of George's handkerchief, Ignatius' head would smash against the wooden tabletop.*)

GEORGE (*sensing that very soon Ignatius will give up the ghost, slyly, the alcoholic loosens the noose and asks Virgil to burden his conscience with the murder*): Now, give the animal a whack over the head... But a hefty one, so that daddy will know he's taken his medicine! ...

(*Virgil hesitates. Struggling against his reluctance, Virgil raises his hand, grasping the iron bar, higher and higher. His arm is trembling from the strain.*)

WALDO (*speaking to himself, as though his narration of what he can see happening in front of him absorbed his entire attention and were by no means intended merely to goad Virgil on*): Nevertheless I must admit... Claudia swept all the dustbin men and loiterers outside with her broom... She aired the flat... She didn't even put on her secret perfume... And it would be a pity, now that she's dressed up in her bikini, with her red slippers... Which she always puts on only for her husband...

(*The weapon, at the end of the raised arm, judders more and more violently, reflecting the struggle in Virgil's heart.*)

CAIUS (*still under the influence of the group of conspirators, into whose ranks he has invited himself, unconcernedly heightens the pressure on Virgil*): There's a squeak at the door and someone is snitching on you... Look at Virgil! He promised someone he'd smash a head in like breaking an eggshell, from a gigantic basket of eggs. And, even though he risks never being able to go home, to your house. Look, he's not going to smash it in!

WALDO: And then Claudia says to him...

GEORGE (*spits out his handkerchief. Although he hasn't really understood the spirit of the story constructed by Waldo and Caius, he hastens to make his own contribution*): Fuck it!

WALDO: No… she'll say to him: Inform my husband and master, who is out shopping, that the steak, which I've made for him and him alone, is in the oven… The wine is in the fridge… And, unhappy woman that I am, the only thing I'm lacking, so that we can sit down to dinner together, is merely those items that are still in the shops, those all important nuts of his! …

(*The double entendre contained in Waldo's words at last makes up Virgil's mind. Pushed from every side, he acts.*)

VIRGIL (*mutters as he strikes*): One basket… Two baskets… Three baskets…

(*Virgil wallops Ignatius once, twice, three times on the back of the head. After the first two blows, Caius joins him and hits Ignatius with his iron bar. George unwraps his now blood-soaked handkerchief from around the Catholic priest's neck. He scrunches it up and inserts it back in his mouth, without neglecting, towards the end, to thump the Catholic priest a few times in the upper part of his body.*

Ignatius is now dead. His head is a bloody mass. Clumps of hair, splinters of bone, bits of brain, and splatters of blood are strewn everywhere. The butchered head and shoulders drop onto the tabletop.

Some of the persons seated close by flick off the organic particles that have landed on their clothes or exposed flesh.)

KIRILL (*having approvingly witnessed the murder of Ignatius, begins to speak, using, once again, both of his voices in turn, a sign of the presence of the two completely different persons inhabiting his body. Sometimes, Kirill's two voices address each other, question each other, answer each other, do or do not provide explanations to each other, confronting each other, for the most part, with deep hostility*).

– (*The first line in the following exchange is spoken by Kirill with VOICE NUMBER 1, his old voice, that of the dementia sufferer*): You went up to my motorcycle…

– (*Kirill answers himself, but with VOICE NUMBER 2, interrupting VOICE*

NUMBER 1 with laughter and diabolical grunting): Hurgh! … Hurgh! … Hurgh! … Hurgh! …

– (*Kirill continues with VOICE NUMBER 1*): … And you've killed them again… What good did it do you, evil man, to make this man's nose bleed so much?

– (*Kirill, VOICE NUMBER 2 answers VOICE NUMBER 1 with a certain amiability*): That idiot (*with a jerk of his head, Kirill indicates Waldo*) warned him not to fiddle with the clock. The other idiot (*Kirill points a finger at the corpse of Ignatius*) was an unbeliever and didn't believe him. And he fiddled… He didn't even need to make his nose bleed. Because he didn't even have a nose…

(*Paranasius, Amanda and Zaid remain on the bench, although they have instinctively drawn away from the blood shed by Ignatius. The three religious leaders follow events as they unfold with the utmost attention, but avoid intervening in any way or uttering a single word.*
    Caius lends Virgil a helping hand to remove the black vestments from the cadaver of the Roman-Catholic priest.)

CAIUS (*to Virgil*): Wear his clothes on top of yours, so that Olympia will think you're a Hindu… Because I, when I want to escape from here, am going to dress up as a cockroach!

PICA (*to Marcel, referring to what Kirill has said, with VOICE NUMBER 2, about Waldo*): Who's an idiot?

VIRGIL (*amazed, to Caius, continuing to undress Ignatius' corpse*): You still don't want to escape from here?! …

MARCEL (*answering Pica*): The devil that has entered Kirill said that Waldo is an idiot.

CAIUS (*answering Virgil*): I've escaped from here three times: once for Marcel, once for the Prince, once instead of Pica… Today I'm going to escape for Raphael… But when I want to come back home to my house, instead of me, I'll dress up as a cockroach! …

(*Virgil and Caius, perfunctorily assisted by George, remove the last priestly vestments from the corpse of Ignatius. After a very short moment of hesitation, Virgil hastens to pull on the garments of the Catholic priest over his pyjamas. Following a discreet sign from Waldo, George offers no opposition to Ignatius' clothes being appropriated only by Virgil. However hurriedly Virgil tries to dress up, he has managed only to put on the top half of the Catholic costume. He is still hurrying. He is dressed only in the black jacket – on back to front – and in his ancient pyjama bottoms.*)

VIRGIL (*asks Caius, while he struggles to smooth out the last creases in the black Catholic tunic*): In which of the clothes of the holies is it easier for you to get back home?

CAIUS: The simplest thing, so as to get through the walls, hide from Olympia, and get rid of these three priests, who haven't got a clue whether God exists or not, would be to dress up as a cockroach… but a motorcyclist would do just as well. Or the way you're dressed up, as a rabbi…

(*Virgil seems very surprised and sad to hear that he looks like a rabbi. He tries to examine his clothing, to gauge his image as reflected in certain objects not at all suited for use as a mirror. His disquiet, concretised in the fact that he might look like a rabbi, added to the horror that he might, at any time, be prevented from escaping, makes him overcome the obstacle and pull on Ignatius' Catholic trousers over his own. He examines himself again. Now he looks completely different… He feels that it is highly likely that he has attained a sufficiently elevated level of elegance to be able to escape.*)

VIRGIL (*to Caius*): Do I escape now?

WALDO (*he has lately swallowed, without even blinking, the insult hurled at him by Kirill with VOICE NUMBER 2, followed by the disrespectful comments of Marcel. He has perfectly reined in his temper. At last, he addresses Virgil*): It's not only hygienic but also very courageous on your part to kill Catholics. Especially given that, according to the rumours, the servants of this faith are the most malicious and vengeful individuals in the world… (*To Paranasius*): Isn't that right, Underbelly of Hell?

PARANASIUS (about Ignatius): Let the devils play dice with his puny soul and that of his mother, father! … Was it not he who leapt from the stable of Christ and fled to the Unclean One?!

GEORGE (because of the handkerchief stuffed in his mouth, dumbly gesticulates to the effect that, "Yes. He leapt"): Moohaha!

PARANASIUS: Did he not bow his knee to the Vatican Idol, to the Pope?!

VIRGIL (so that none of them will change their minds and ask for the costume back): Oho! How he bowed his knee! …

PARANASIUS: And did he not entice our Holy Orthodox People – may the crows devour him! – to his papist faith?!

MARCEL: As though we were your Holy Orthodox People! As though we rejoiced like you, ugly, when that lot prepared brain stew for him with their crow bars?! …

PICA: I love stew. But it's not like we love the stewmakers.

WALDO (turning his gaze to the imam): But what is the opinion of your holiness, Zaid, about our brother Ignatius.

(*Automatically, almost all the heads in the ward turn towards Zaid. Their curiosity is also heightened by the paucity of the words spoken by the devotee of the teachings of Islam during the course of the Festival of Meetings up to now. Zaid is dignified in his bearing and brims with unaffected ceremony. His way of speaking is direct and decisive, but radiates an inner serenity much less specific than that revealed by Amanda in his comportment.*)

ZAID: "Our brother Ignatius" is not at all my brother! He was merely a highly dangerous scoundrel… Like all infidels…

GEORGE (*the gesture with the handkerchief. As though elucidating what, in his opinion, Zaid wished to say*): An ox!

ZAID (*looking at George with rage and disgust, barely refraining from attacking him but then ignoring the interruption, the imam continues what he has been saying, acquiring the inflections of a sermon*): Allah teaches us that all infidels must first be instructed and then invited to convert to Islam… If they refuse, war is waged against them. If they surrender without a fight, they may be exempted from conversion, but they will pay a tribute… You can hardly imagine – when the deadline came to pay the tribute – how many cunning tricks and delays this scoundrel employed!

LUPU: How is that?! Ignatius used to pay you tribute?

ZAID: He was a rascal, but he also loved his life exceedingly much. And so, in the end, he would pay.

THE PRINCE (*to Zaid*): And where did he procure the money to pay you the tribute?

AMANDA: From me… He always used to insist on the aspect that if I liked suffering anyway… After kidnapping some children from my native region, he went as far as to keep saying that he could inure them to such evil deeds that the infants, in their next existence, would not even be reincarnated as pigs, but directly as stones… "And what do I care?!" I would ask him. "If this is their Karma?!" … But after much talking, because he kept disturbing me in my sessions of mortification, I used to sign those papers and pay his tribute.

CAIUS: What, you pay it for him?

GEORGE (*the handkerchief*): But why? He kicked your pennies out of the house?

LUPU: Weren't you – owooo! – a mendicant monk?!

MARCEL (*to Zaid*): For such a big bandit, who leaves ten wives pregnant and doesn't even take care of the children, why didn't you demand the tribute from him directly, baldy?

(*Zaid is deeply offended by the familiarity with which Marcel addresses him. Once more, he barely manages to stop himself rising from his place and teaching the insolent Marcel a brutal lesson.*)

MARCEL (*continuing, with the same lack of inhibition, to Zaid*): Why are you giving me such a dirty look? (*Showing the rag "baby" nestling at his breast*): You wouldn't be wanting to make a Tartar or a janissary out of him, would you?

AMANDA (*explains to Marcel, with the utmost amiability and lack of resentment*): His plan stipulates that he collect as much tribute as possible. Separate from Ignatius, separate from myself, separate from anyone else whatsoever… But I do not pay tribute to Zaid directly, because he has not concluded all the formalities for launching a "holy war" against me.

MARCEL (*becomes suspicious, but still towards Amanda. He examines the features of the Buddhist monk's face, then communicating to Zaid worriedly*): It's a bit like he has the mug of a Turkish horseman! …

WALDO: Now we are all clear about the wretched character of our father Ignatius and because we have established…

VIRGIL (*is overwhelmed by such a powerful frenzy that he no longer feels inhibited, but invincible and unstoppable, precisely because of his Catholic raiment. Moving more and more briskly, he has reached the middle of the ward, at the very spot where the preaching chair and carpet are set up. He is rocked by a tremor that transfigures him*): I'm leaving now! … Now I feel an indescribable power to pass through the walls, like a sword through a pat of butter! … What would you like me to pass on to your grandmother, if she's still alive, Zoli?

ZOLI (*he is amazed, but, from the agitation that takes hold of him, he demonstrates that he has understood the words Virgil has addressed to him. He seems to be searching for an answer. He replies, lost*): … I don't know.

GEORGE (*pulls the handkerchief out of his mouth and is about to utter one of his low vulgarities*): Tell her…

VIRGIL (*interrupts and pays no heed to George*): Claudia, my wife: what should I pass on to your wife, dear Pica?

WALDO (*following the thread of the discussion with a hidden satisfaction*): We have established how malicious some Catholics can be…

PICA (*with a tenderness surprising precisely because it is coming from him*): That I would die, only to be able to kiss her again! … (*Remembering a detail, and suddenly worried, also to Virgil*): Listen, my wife is a lamppost in Victory Plaza… Tell your wife not to break its neck. If she clambers up her… To have a coffee there, just the two girls…

VIRGIL (*he pauses for the last time before legging it through the walls. Turning around to a certain patient, he says to him, more in reproach than vengefully*): But if I'd asked you… Whether your younger sister… Little Adriana… Whether she'd like. Me to make love to her, Waldo?!

WALDO: …But, as far as I can see, it doesn't even cross your mind how vengeful those Catholics can prove to be!

PICA (*to Virgil, still referring to Adriana, Waldo's younger sister, mentioned previously*): Don't touch her! …Who knows what love she thinks it is. And we'll find ourselves with a little Waldo upon us…

CAIUS (*from his series of "oblique" questions*): Then why don't we invite her and the lamppost to slide down and break their necks?

VIRGIL (*once more on the alert due to his imminent escape attempt. He anxiously moves towards the part of the ward he is talking about*): Through the secret little door here… behind the filing cabinets from where their holinesses climbed out, I'll slip through. As for the steak, nicely browned by Claudia just for me, I'm not even going to touch…

PICA: Don't throw it away! … Who knows what kind of madman you think you are. And they'll bring you back, yet again, they'll tie you up, here...

VIRGIL: The drop of wine, chilled in the fridge especially for me, I'm not even going to taste...

GEORGE (*although he has removed the handkerchief from his mouth, for a second he cannot speak, because of his disgust at what Virgil has just said. Then*): Then why should we get upset at the woman?! I'll go and drink it myself.

VIRGIL (*he speaks while attempting to insert his body, protected by the Catholic clothes, into the narrow space between the first filing cabinet and the wall, in order then to go straight through the wall*): Only in the bedroom... Like a knight, from the times of your highness, Prince... (*He makes a polite gesture towards the Prince*): I shall dismount... My forehead on Claudia's breast I shall rest... And I shall... I shall tell the story... Oho! What stories I shall tell! ... (*Although he has not yet reached the little door of salvation, which he suspects lies behind the filing cabinet, he calmly goes on trying to squeeze his body between the metal cabinet and the plaster.*) After that... naturally. My hand on the telephone I shall place. I'll call and inform them all. The rulers of the land, in the first place! ... Bulldozers for them to send... These cursed walls, under their caterpillar tracks, for them to destroy... Like bits of candle, for them to crush the bars... And, if I cannot save you in the heavens, like only their holinesses know how to do. At least in the wonderful world outside, I shall free absolutely all of you here!

GEORGE (*while the rest of the room are for a moment carried away by Virgil's story, the alcoholic frees his mouth. And he addresses Virgil with perfidious grovelling*): Of course... But before you... (*It is obvious that he can barely refrain from blurting out something obscene. Then, with even heavier grovelling.*) The bottle of wine, which you were saying... that you're not going to drink it yourself...

(*Virgil does not answer George, either yes or no. Virgil continues to bump himself, in a slow rhythm, against the ingress to the space into which he would like to fit, so that he might then pass through the secret little door he supposes to be in the wall. He does not manage to slip through, but he does not lose heart. On the contrary. The ardour he puts into his escape attempt increases. With the utmost zeal, he tries to thrust his body at various angles into the gap between the back of the filing cabinet and the wall. He scrabbles at the plaster with his nails, trying to gain a purchase.)*

WALDO (*watching his efforts with curiosity, but also a tenderness that seems to break his heart*): Where are you going, Virgil?

VIRGIL (*not ceasing his exertions in the period that immediately follows. Thus, he still has his back to Waldo. He answers him with slight mockery*): I'm off home for a while… (*Simply*): To my wife.

WALDO (*with the same tenderness and overwhelming astonishment*): What wife?

VIRGIL (*bitter irony*): I thought you said you knew her?!

WALDO: If you're talking about Claudia, why are you bringing up the subject, when you know how touchy you are? …And if you're talking about someone you imagine you're married to: what wife?

VIRGIL: Mightn't it be her, the one you had a jealous fit over when I told you about her wedding?!

WALDO: No. There was no way it could have been… Because, listen, this is what the medical experts have concluded about you! (*He feels around. He seems to find what he is looking for. Once more, he extracts from the foam innards of his mattress his all-too-familiar psychiatry textbook. He flicks through it as he speaks, until he reckons he has found the right page.*) Don't you think you're suffering from certain… (*he pretends to be reading from the psychiatry textbook*) … "encephalic illnesses… Impossibly nauseating, especially for those very close to you… Which when they strike you, they throw you to the ground, regardless of where you are. You lose consciousness… They make you writhe. Vomit. Urinate. Foam at the mouth. Bite your tongue, as though you were biting a piece of plasticine… And when you come out of your deep coma, of course you don't remember absolutely anything about what you have been doing. You even swear that you've filled your surroundings with nothing but beautiful deeds?! …"

VIRGIL (*continuing to scrabble to open a way through the wall*): I may well have that. Since you started reading to me from the medical experts and I became Catholic, I've had it less…

WALDO: Good. But what about when you fell ill with these unbearable illnesses. How long have you been ill? … Since this morning? Or ever since birth?!

MARCEL (*very impressed, to Virgil*): You were born? You have a very slim waist for a priest who has just been born.

GEORGE (*takes the handkerchief out of his mouth and answers Waldo's question as though Virgil were answering*): Ever since…

VIRGIL (*he answers Marcel's question. He uses the same tone of bonhomie and jokiness, and he does not even interrupt the efforts he is making to escape through the wall. Gradually, he moves away from the area of the wall at which he has been scrabbling. He sets off to explore. He examines other portions of the walls. He spreads around him goodwill, confidence and excitement*): I've done all kinds of sports. And I was on a diet for a long time.

WALDO (*allowing a short pause for effect, in order to gain an even greater importance for the words he is about to utter*): So, if you've been ill ever since birth, why are you surprised that the Catholic proved so vengeful? … You shattered his skull, you thought that you had made friends…

GEORGE (*the handkerchief*): You splattered his brains, you thought he'd forgive you, as though he was your mammy…

KIRILL (*speaking with VOICE NUMBER 2, the demonic one*): But in fact…

WALDO: But in fact, as soon as you killed him, he, all in one breath. And, why don't we admit it, and you left him…

KIRILL (*with VOICE NUMBER 2*) … stark …

WALDO: … naked… That's how you left him.

KIRILL (with VOICE NUMBER 2): He ran all the way to the maternity ward of your old neighbourhood.

WALDO: He obtained a medical certificate that since the exact moment of your birth you have been suffering from this illness, this serious and repulsive illness.

KIRILL (with VOICE NUMBER 2): And he tucked, if I can put it like that, the certificate under his arm.

CAIUS (he has once more fallen under the influence that the group of conspirators intermittently exert over him): If he climbed two flights of stairs up to your flat.

WALDO: Where…

KIRILL (with VOICE NUMBER 2): Ignatius revealed, at length, to the woman you call your wife. That…

WALDO: Because of the terrible diagnosis you were born with…

KIRILL (with VOICE NUMBER 2): In the eyes of the Church, the marriage between you had no way of being valid…

WALDO: Or even more concisely: that the free-and-easy Claudia was never genuinely your wife!

VIRGIL (it is his turn to start losing his good spirits. For the first time, during this period, he stops searching the walls. He turns, bewildered, to those in the ward. He intuits more than he understands the evil into which he is about to be precipitated. Still smiling, he blurts out): What wife?!

CAIUS (amazed and, once more, in good faith, without irony, to Virgil): But didn't you say that you know her?!

WALDO (*to Paranasius*): If a man, incapable of making the decision to marry, marries, through diabolical wiles, a healthy woman. What do your holy books say, Underbelly of Hell?

PARANASIUS: The Holy Christian Church, my son, reviles the deceiver. It dissolves the unsuitable marriages of both. It straightaway releases the woman, it leaves her free, unfettering her from her troth.

(*Virgil is beginning to understand what they are talking about. All of a sudden he goes limp. He pales. He is sweating. Then he feels how the epileptic aura is coming over him – a transformation which precedes the epileptic fit proper and which lasts from a few seconds to a minute, a minute and a half. However, the epileptic aura is experienced by the sufferer as a much longer period of time, and as an insupportable immixture in the intimacy of his consciousness.*)

WALDO: "But how can you abandon a woman – a woman now left without any purpose in the world – a woman so free and so frolicsome? …"

KIRILL (*with VOICE NUMBER 2*): … The soul of Ignatius said to itself. (*Afterwards addressing George, making a sign for him to continue.*) And as he was fretting, albeit still…

GEORGE (*understands what is demanded of him. He removes his handkerchief*): Bare-arsed…

KIRILL (*with VOICE NUMBER 2*): Just as he had scuttled out of here.

WALDO: A tablecloth around the thighs of his soul, he wrapped himself in…

GEORGE: A Catholic, stiff enough to break rock, from them in the… (*he whispers*) community, he asked for…

WALDO: And without further ado, rectifying the defect. In the Roman-Catholic tradition and abiding by all the rules of the clergy: the two of them genuinely got married! … (*Looking towards a group of his fellow patients.*) Tell me a Catholic name!

MARCEL: Ignatius…

WALDO: Not you. (*Addressing Lupu*): You!

LUPU: Pope Boniface the Eighth.

WALDO (*smiling*): Alright.

KIRILL (*with VOICE NUMBER 2*): Not only should you not go near her forever and ever. But even…

GEORGE (*an obscene gesture*): On the contrary…

WALDO: You should even stay away from her.

KIRILL (*with VOICE NUMBER 2*): That is, away from your usual bed, further away… Maybe under the sink. You should move.

WALDO: Or, to quote her exactly…

GEORGE (*the handkerchief. Making an effort to speak in a sophisticated manner*): "Kindly inform the rotter…"

(*All the things he has heard have surpassed Virgil's limits of endurance. A single moment sufficed for Virgil to take to heart and believe the innuendos the conspirators have besmirched him with. And in the end, Virgil is slain. Virgil falls to the ground, prey to a fearful epileptic fit. None of what accompanies the peak of such a crisis seems to circumvent the patient.*

Instinctively, most of the patients gather around him. Curious and amused, the conspirators, delay dealing him the coup-de-grace with their iron bars, so that they can observe whether Virgil takes his own life during his epileptic fit. In order to help the epileptic, Marcel, Pica and Raphael try to protect him from the worst wounds his spectacular convulsions might cause him.

Unexpectedly, however, the intensity of the epileptic fit diminishes, to the disappointment of the first group and the joy of the second. Observing that, almost out of the blue, Virgil is now at rest on the floor, Marcel, Pica and Raphael snatch him from under the noses of the conspirators, lifting him up, unsteadily and with difficulty, carrying him and depositing him in his own bed.

Without setting out to, Marcel, Pica, Raphael and Caius form a protective wall with their bodies around the inert body of Virgil. This hindering position rather disconcerts the conspirators, weakening, for the moment, their eagerness to rush upon Virgil and deal, without further ado, the coup-de-grace. A brief lull ensues.)

GEORGE (*the handkerchief. To Marcel, Pica, Raphael and Caius, massed around Virgil's bed. He addresses them with a mixture of friendliness and cunning*): At least take those togs off him, so that we can give them to Virgil's orphans for them to sell. So that the poor things can at least have something to drink! ...

CAIUS (*naïvely and "obliquely"*): What orphans?! (*And referring to Virgil*): Can't you see that it's only now that he's gathering all his strength to escape?

KIRILL (*with VOICE NUMBER 2*): Caius, darling, in order to escape, first of all he has to be washed! ...But look at him! He's riddled with more devils than a rotten apple teeming with maggots...

WALDO (*looking meaningfully at Paranasius*): Is there a problem, your holiness?

KIRILL (*with VOICE NUMBER 1, the demented voice, referring to what VOICE NUMBER 2 has just said*): Did you hear him?! ... Don't tell me you didn't hear him. He alone says no one is allowed. To teem in you. And to throw you off your motorcycle!

PARANASIUS (*answering Waldo*): The rite of extreme unction?

WALDO (*to Paranasius*): I would not even have dreamt that it could be omitted.

PARANASIUS (*to Waldo again*): The Prayers of St Basil the Great?

WALDO: As you say, Underbelly.

PARANASIUS (it is obvious he can hardly wait to read them. But he pretends to hesitate, in order to give an even greater importance to his intervention, in which he is going to read the Prayers of St Basil the Great, in order to drive out the evil spirits that haunt Virgil): They are too powerful, father…

KIRILL (with VOICE NUMBER 2. Aside. Amusedly): Powerful my arse! … The last time, when they read them to me, they tickled me and sent me to sleep, so much so that I almost fell out of the man.

GEORGE (the handkerchief. The same friendliness and cunning as before. To Caius in particular, but it is understood that he is also addressing Marcel, Pica and Raphael): The priest is giving him a shower in his prayers. He's washing off the devils. And after that, he can piss off where he likes.

KIRILL (with VOICE NUMBER 2): So, your holiness, you chant the psalms so beautifully… And where need be (*he points to himself*) even the innocent accompany you.

(Under the pretext that he is going to heal the epileptic, Paranasius is thrust forward and escorted by the group of conspirators to the side of Virgil's bed, thereby displacing Marcel, Pica and Raphael.
　　Caius draws back a little, stands still, and then, under the preponderant influence of the moment, he joins the actions of the conspirators once more.
　　With Paranasius at their head, who advances towards Virgil holding his miracle-working icon, the group of conspirators approaches, not empty handed, but each holding, besides his iron bar, one or another of the liturgical items with which the priest is endowed. Kirill swings the censer, in which frankincense is burning, and carries under his arm two hefty tomes. George is shaking a receptacle with holy water and has not forgotten to fetch the consecrated oil.)

PARANASIUS (holding the icon, he intones parts of the mass, which he knows by heart, to Virgil): "Mother of God, Ever-Virgin Mary, Precious Veil of Protection. Haven and wall. Stair and tower. Have mercy upon and heal this afflicted man, for to thee he hath fled…" (*With a changed tone of voice, also to Virgil, who, in bed, is giving signs of life, tossing from side to side*): Kiss the miracle-working icon, you piece of filth!

VIRGIL (writhes once more, but with spasms that are less violent than the convulsions of epilepsy. He speaks in a voice that possesses his usual timbre, but which seems to be used by another creature or many other creatures that have made their dwelling inside his body. It is as though these inner creatures of his are talking to him, Virgil): It's no use you writhing, we're still not going to leave here... We've brought down the whole of hell on you... We are in charge! We are an occupying regime. We are a mass meeting. We are legion. We are a bus terminal. How can we go away from here?! ...Where shall we make our camp? Where shall we make our camp?

RAPHAEL: Make your camp in the desert.

MARCEL: In a barren place and where you won't disturb anyone.

VIRGIL (Speaking in the same way as before): No. Because there is no discotheque there.

CAIUS (without malice and "obliquely"): Better we send them off to the cinema.

GEORGE (the handkerchief. For a moment he gives up torturing Virgil, in favour of a transaction that seems to him more advantageous): Yes. Come out of there and then enter that bone-idle Olympia and get her to buy us a vat of medicinal spirit.

CAIUS (thoughtfully): It's still better at the cinema.

GEORGE (continuing what he has begun to say): ... And bring that medicinal alcohol over here to my dick. Which like an elephant will suck it up with its trunk all at once!

PARANASIUS (hastens to resume the chanting of the mass, displeased at the length of the interruption): "... Mother of the Creator of all, find the benevolence. And with thy prayers deliver this afflicted man from bitter suffering."

VIRGIL (the same): We are in the kidneys. We are in the brain. We are in the guts. We are in the throat. We are in the strands of the hair. We are in the knees. We are in the pyjamas.

PARANSIUS: Evil spirits, come out from him!

MARCEL: He's not wearing pyjamas.

KIRILL (*with VOICE NUMBER 2, unexpectedly begins to celebrate the mass alongside Paranasius, chanting, but also censing*): Come on out of him, you evil spirits… "Ever-praised, immaculate, Virgin Mary take pity on him that has been anointed with holy unguent and have mercy on him, thy servant."

PARANASIUS (*looking first of all at Kirill in surprise and annoyance. Then, weighing up the two options, he prefers to continue chanting, celebrating mass alongside Kirill, rather than no longer to be at the centre of attention*): "All-merciful Lord, who with thy untold love. Didst receive unction from the dissolute woman, take pity on Thy servant."

VIRGIL (*as before*): We are in the lungs. We are in the bones. We are in the mouth… Don't you see you're dying? Get to a hospital, Virgil, because you're dying! …We are in the bone marrow. We are in the whites of the eyes. We are in the blood. We are where no mind can guess.

LUPU (*who has not aligned himself to either group. Because of his itching skin, he is continually crawling around the ward on all fours*): A-woo! Who sent you?

VIRGIL (*the same*): Madam McBishop, Claudia's neighbour, she sent us.

RAPHAEL: Go and set up camp at Madam McBishop's then.

VIRGIL (*the same*): Madam McBishop is now dead. She's now knitting sweaters in hell, Madam McBishop… Come on, Virgil, let's take a walk to hell, to Madam McBishop! Because it was she who cast a spell on you with the water used to bathe a corpse.

PICA (*in connexion to the ceremony that is unfolding beneath his eyes and the* answers given by Virgil, senses that something is not quite right. He tries with all his might to oppose it, using only his insignificant, ordinary, human powers. He wants to say something. But he can't find what. In desperation, he finally repeats the words that have so often been uttered in the ward. And which all of a sudden take on a new significance): "… If I die a little, wake me up!"

VIRGIL (the same): You're stupid for dying. Listen to us for a little and you're saved. Don't touch the steak. Don't touch Claudia. He's stupid for dying.

PICA (as before, opposing it. And answering with what he thinks would be the most appropriate thing for Virgil to answer): "… Nip my ballpoint and I'll rise from the dead! …"

PARANASIUS (hastens to resume the service): "Saint Panteleimon, holy passion-bearer and healer, pray to all-merciful God to grant forgiveness for the sins of the soul of the afflicted Virgil."

KIRILL (with VOICE NUMBER 2, accompanying Paranasius): "Unmercenary physician saints and miracle-workers, search our infirmities. In gift you received, in gift give unto us."

VIRGIL (the same. With even greater writhing): Satan has planted his heel upon my soul. My mind has been bound by Satan… In vain you writhe… In vain he writhes.

PARANASIUS (still to Virgil, seeking to obtain from him a declaration favourable to the Church, which he, Paranasius, represents): Say after me: "Only righteous Orthodox Christians find salvation. Only you, Orthodox priests, are heeded by God. By Holy Unction, by the Holy Icons, by the Holy Cross, by the Holy Gospels, by the Holy Relics, by the hands and the vestments of the holy priests we are most terribly affrighted. The devils of the sects are ours. The sects come from us."

KIRILL (with VOICE NUMBER 2, continuing the service, chanting and censing Virgil): "Holy Virgin, receiving the hymns and prayers offered by thy servants, deliver him who through us flees to thy divine veil of protection."

VIRGIL (the same): Come out of him commandant, and let us follow after you! …This lot may be from the greatest stage show ever, but they've bored us to death. Come on, let's find some writers. Let's go over to Daniel's to drink fruit syrup with Madam McBishop.

PARANASIUS (drawing even closer to Virgil's ear): Also say: "Our greatest rancour is against you, Orthodox priests! You are the only ones who are truly holy… Aren't they going to name you the Great Saint Paranasius the Great?! And shouldn't all those present convert to holy and right-believing Orthodoxy, in order to save their souls?!

KIRILL (with VOICE NUMBER 2, still chanting and censing): "Mother of God, let God have mercy on this suffering man…"

PARANASIUS (continuing to advise Virgil as to what he should assert in his next cries): … Let the Hindu convert to Orthodoxy… (*He pauses, hesitating. Then he speaks to the effect that the Roman-Catholic would not even deserve to become an Orthodox Christian*): The Catholic, no… Let the Buddhist convert to Orthodoxy. Let the Mahommedan convert to Orthodoxy.

ZAID (to Paranasius, as though in jest. But still with the same haughty bearing, and accompanying his warning with a brief gesture towards the dagger in his belt): Watch out!

PARANASIUS (still to Virgil): …But he ought to. But the greatest sorrow in the world would be for us, the spirits of darkness… As I have instructed you, say it!

VIRGIL (the same): Evacuate the bus terminal, because almost all of them are ours. Let's take our belongings and bore a hole some place else.

GEORGE (the handkerchief. Also chanting, the best he knows how, in derision): Let Olympia convert to Orthodoxy.

PARANASIUS (with the icon in his hands, he takes up the thread of the service once more): "With Thy abundant grace, O Christ, and with the unction of Thy priests, wash away, O Lord, the pain and the wounds of this man…"

KIRILL (*with VOICE NUMBER 2, this time he effectively begins to celebrate mass side by side with Paranasius, taking up the words from his mouth and uttering alternately – now him, now the Orthodox priest – the same phrase of the service*): "… who is afflicted…"

PARANASIUS (*carrying on the chant from where Kirill left off, with VOICE NUMBER 2*): "… by the sufferings of the passions…"

KIRILL (*with VOICE NUMBER 2, continuing what Paranasius is saying*): "… so that, finding salvation…" (*from this point he begins to add, unobserved, of his own volition, new phrases to the service, which he, with VOICE NUMBER 2, and Paranasius have alternately been chanting*): Right under the bed of Claudia…

PICA (*uneasy. He senses danger. From his place, by one of the beds, to Virgil*): Don't answer them!

KIRILL (*with VOICE NUMBER 2, as before*): … and she and her new husband made him end up… Bursting his eardrums from the noise the two lunatics incessantly make! (*Resuming the consecrated phrasing of the service, which he chants together with Paranasius*): "… And let him glorify Thee in thanks."

(*Virgil alternates writhing with periods of calm.*

A new period of calm. All of a sudden, coinciding with the end of the latest line spoken by Kirill, writhing like a headless chicken, Virgil springs out of bed. His writhing is part normal walking, part convulsion.

Virgil first rushes at Paranasius, who is nearest – in the space between beds – of those blocking his path. He pushes Paranasius. He snatches the icon. All three fall to the ground: Virgil, the icon, and Paranasius.

Kirill and George bend over to immobilise the epileptic, but Virgil is once more on his feet and writhing. Virgil shoulders Kirill in the chest, becomes entangled in the chains of the censer and drags Kirill to the ground. Struggling. A scrum of arms and legs. Nonetheless, the first to get up is, surprisingly, Virgil. George too is surprised. The alcoholic takes two or three steps backward, making way for the epileptic. Virgil walks, shudders, falls, gets up, walks. He does not reach the wall through which he had planned to escape. In the middle of the ward, in the place which had been used for the sermons of the four religious teachers, Virgil falls heavily, with a loud thud. His body is shaken by one last convulsion. A dry twitch of catastrophe. Then, for a long while, Virgil's body remains motionless. Likewise, Pica and Marcel, followed by Caius, remain motionless after they approach and examine Virgil's body. They turn him face upwards on the floor. They raise the upper part of his torso. One of them rests Virgil's neck on his knee.)

PARANASIUS (he has straightened robes, rumpled by his having been toppled to the ground. Solemn. He is referring to the demons supposed to have been dwelling inside Virgil, which he had been trying to drive out): ...They have come out.

WALDO: Yes. But he was also killed. He slashed his veins, Underbelly, on the glass of the icon, and went off to the cinema with the devils.

END OF ACT TWO

ACT THREE

SET AND PRELIMINARIES

The same ward. The same number of beds, lined up in the same way. Neither the cauldron with the dirty clothes nor the gigantic metal box in which crockery, cutlery, leftovers and other filth was deposited can now be seen.

In front of the wall at the back of the stage there have appeared four booths, closed off from the rest of the stage by sheets, and which looks like four tents. On the four tents are pinned four sheets of paper, on each of which a word is inscribed. Looking from the audience, from left to right, on the first tent is inscribed the word "CEMETERY". On the second tent is inscribed "PRISON". On the third tent is inscribed "GOVERNMENT". And on the fourth tent is inscribed "HEAVEN".

    At the beginning of Act Three, Marcel, Pica, Lupu, *the* Prince, Raphael *and* Zoli *can be seen in the ward. With the exception of Lupu, who is crawling around the floor on all fours, all five patients are in their beds.*

    The story of the Prince *awakens profound interest in the other patients.*

THE PRINCE: … But the womb of the worthy woman became heavy. And after the allotted interval of nine months had elapsed, she gave birth, at an interval of just a few minutes between each, to three enchanting babies of the male sex… The first of them received from the fates the most distinguished gift a man can receive. The second boy was endowed with the gift of obtaining the richest harvests in the world. And as they did not have anything left to offer the youngest brother…

RAPHAEL (*overcoming his shyness*): Forgive me, Prince. What exactly did the first of the babies receive?

THE PRINCE: The gift of serving at my court.

MARCEL (*knitting, while he rocks the dandles baby on his knees*): Aha.

THE PRINCE: And to the youngest of the newborn the fates gave the power to see even the spirits that gather around the head of a man.

PICA: How is that?

THE PRINCE: Which is to say, the gift of seeing the unseen. Which is to say, of seeing as though through glass everything that it is impossible for other men to see. "Your Enlightenment, allow me to provide you with some proof," he told me. "Under the floorboards in that corner are there not buried three corpses: one that of a very vigorous man, the other that of a very jealous man, and the third that of a man who was advised that only thus would he be got out of the habit of fiddling with the clock?"

LUPU (*the lupine howl, but somehow as an aside*): Ignatiu-ooo-us!

RAPHAEL: Our good Tănăsîcu.

MARCEL: How could he have got it into his head to trick you about those bodies?

THE PRINCE: "May the heavens strike us down, Highness!" they reported to me. "If more than five laths we had to lift in order to convince ourselves that the enchanted man was telling you the truth."

LUPU: How-oooo could he trick him?

MARCEL: Maybe he thought you were in hospital. That many people wish you ill. What do you think, Prince.

THE PRINCE: "After we unearthed the corpses, we followed the other advice of the seer, Majesty. And, behold, we found three men, who look like priests… here. Tied up. In a tent…" – the voice of your father, Marcel, resounded full of fervour.

MARCEL: What father?

THE PRINCE: Your father. The husband of your mother.

MARCEL (*suspicious*): What mother?

THE PRINCE: "It is true that we too were overly severe, Your Highness. But we would have sunk into the earth for shame, especially when we heard about his illegitimate offspring" – as both your father and your mother complained to me, Marcel.

PICA (*although he is almost convinced that he has understood incorrectly, he cannot stop himself from interrogating Marcel*): You have a spring?

LUPU (*elucidating, in his capacity as history teacher*): No-ooo. Offspring. Children born outside a marriage recognised by the state.

MARCEL (*moving his baby to a place further away from the Prince, continues to question him*): What were they looking for here?

THE PRINCE: Abiding by the duty to worship firstly not the religious representatives but the worldly ruler of the realm, Zoli's parents organised a group…

ZOLI (*probably because he has heard his name uttered, unexpectedly reels off a set of residual, very correct phrases, but it is obvious that he understands absolutely nothing of what he is saying*): In Scotland, McGee and Scott observe that the frequency of manias in women increases in the months of March and April.

MARCEL (*calming down, to the Prince*): And Zoli's mother passed herself off as my mother?

ZOLI: Psychiatric illnesses multiply in periods of increasing temperatures.

RAPHAEL (*out of pity and tenderness decides to pay attention to Zoli*): I think you have a great understanding of the illnesses you mention.

ZOLI (*without reacting to the person addressing him*): And alcoholism breaks out strongly at around the middle of May.

THE PRINCE: … No. Zoli's parents led him to kiss the hand of my uncle and Raphael's aunt… Pica's wife… Your parents, Marcel… Lupu's mother.

Lupu's mother's sister, but also her youngest son, the enchanted man…
Who thus proved to be Lupu's first cousin.

(The majority of those who hear the news of their relatives visiting them in the ward, news communicated by the Prince, are overcome by emotion. They fidget, burst into short series of tics, or micro-gestures of anxiety, they breathe with difficulty. One alone retains his inquisitive disposition.)

MARCEL (just as insistently and curiously, to the Prince): Where were we when all of them burst in here?

LUPU (gravely, but also reflecting the overexcitement about to grip the patients for the next four or five minutes): Maybe they were guillotined. Or clumsy.

THE PRINCE: "The sole purpose of this first visit" – they told me – "is to pay you homage, Highness!" They were terribly worried about not infringing protocol… And you were terribly sleepy.

RAPHAEL (dizzy with joy he does not, however, forget to probe further, asking the Prince about what seems to him to be an omission): Didn't anyone come on behalf of Tanasîcu?

PICA (overwhelmed with emotion, addressing them all, but especially the Prince): You asked them to lie down to sleep next to us!

MARCEL (also to the Prince, but emphatically, not carried away by the emotional state of those around him): Why do you say they visited us, when not a single relative visited us, you bad man?

(Confusion. As they begin to comprehend the question by which Marcel has accused the Prince, there is a wave of psychical tension. First, the group of patients do not even believe Marcel. They look at the Prince, expecting the Prince to contradict him. The Prince's demeanour is that of a man caught unawares, profoundly frightened, whose evil deeds have been discovered when he was least expecting. The group of patients can barely believe that neither Raphael's uncle and aunt, nor Pica's wife, nor Marcel's parents, nor Lupu's mother, aunt and cousin, or any other of their relatives, whose presence they had got used to sensed in the ward,

have come to visit and that there are no signs that they will ever come.

Two effects take place. One is profound discouragement on the part of each. The other is that the wave of gratitude with which the patients had surrounded the Prince now decisively transforms into a wave of aggression. Against the backdrop of the Prince being overcome by an attack of stupor, a few of the patients draw closer to him, feel the need to unburden themselves, and begin to hit him. The first blows are not very hard, remaining mere substitutes for reproach. Contaminated by the action of the others, Zoli strikes with his cup. Lupu's bites draw dangerously close to the Prince's throat. The patients are no more than half worked up. But a lynching could ensue at any moment.

On the other hand, the sheets of the third tent, the one on which "GOVERNMENT" is written, puff out, as though something spectacular were happening within. Two or three minutes before the attack on the Prince, noises that appear to be sensuous female whispers began to emerge from this place. Then muffled male voices can be heard uttering obscene and mocking lines of the following kind: "Who taught you to do that, you bitch?" "Sit down, or you'll get a muscle ache, girly." "Calm down, you've given us as good as you've got." "Go out through this air vent, make a decent woman of yourself, and don't let us catch you around here again, you freak." The words spoken by the male voices can't be made out very well. Moreover, they induce a feeling of menace.

Pause. Motionlessness.

Then, once again, the sheets of the tent puff out, but this time they are also pushed to one side. Exactly at the moment the Prince is in danger of being lynched, the "governors" emerge from the tent into the middle of the ward: George, Caius and Kirill. They are oddly apparelled. Underneath they are still wearing their pyjamas, but on top they are each wearing an item of clothing that once belonged to one of the four religious leaders. To this garb are also added the remains of objects which usually make up part of a doctor's instruments: a stethoscope, a reflectorised mirror attached to the forehead, a rubber hammer for testing reflexes, an apparatus for taking blood pressure, a thermometer, pencils, folders, sheaths of paper etc. The three "governors" walk self-importantly and with preoccupied faces towards the scene of the battle.

They address those who are about to lynch the Prince.)

KIRILL (*speaks with VOICE NUMBER 2 as though he were communicating things beyond any doubt. He refers to the Prince, in connexion with what Marcel has lately accused him of*): He lied about your fathers and uncles coming here to see you… But he didn't lie about your mothers and aunts coming.

CAIUS: The enchanted man didn't come to visit.

GEORGE (*the well-known handkerchief gesture*): He said you were too ugly.

KIRILL (*here and in all the following lines which do not specify any change, with VOICE NUMBER 2*): But your mothers and sisters came…

GEORGE (*the handkerchief*): Who meowed all night…

CAIUS: … Begging us to let them pay their homage to us…

GEORGE (*the handkerchief*): … And for us to agree to drink their bottles of perfume…

KIRILL: … And for us – both our master and ourselves – to take pity on you and to make you better!

(*The interruption of the three "governors" has halted the corporal punishment being administered to the Prince. At the moment in which the "governors" begin to speak, the blows stop. In addition, without being explicitly requested to do so, the Prince's attackers each return and climb into their beds. The attackers are still out of breath because of their exertions during the beating and, with a mixture of the most divers feelings, they cannot take their eyes off George, Caius, and Kirill.*)

CAIUS: And so the first person we're going to make better will be…

KIRILL (*nonchalantly indicates the first person he sets eyes on. He points at Pica*): You.

CAIUS (*because none of the three "governors" is concerned about designating any patient in particular, he for one allows himself to alter Kirill's choice and points at the Prince, the one who seems to be in the worst physical shape*): Or you.

GEORGE (*the gesture with the handkerchief*): Look. (*Out of a spirit of contradiction, he too feels the need to change the selection. His index finger travels*

up and down the six patients cowering in their beds and then, suddenly and
without motive, he decides as though by lot. The lot he casts falls upon Lupu.)
We're going to begin the training by making you get better.

(*All three having agreed upon this final choice, the "governors" surround Lupu's
bed, with the demeanour of medical staff. Disoriented and obedient, Lupu allows
himself to be stretched out on his back. The other five patients in the beds follow
the unfolding events with contradictory reactions, but with general relief that they
have not been chosen.*

*A consultation ensues. Lupu is examined, made to execute various movements,
urged to respond summarily, preferably "yes" or "no", to the medical questions.
Captivated by the procedure, Lupu reacts docilely. He no longer even howls, but
merely whimpers now and then.*)

KIRILL (*speaks impersonally, more to himself, as he carries out the consultation*):
Hallucinations, of a sensorial epileptic kind… Secondary disturbances of
delirium.

CAIUS (*with the same concentrated air, takes part in the consultation and
makes brief notes on some sheets of paper*): Expression of indifference to his
surroundings…

KIRILL (*the same as before*): Disorganisation of psychical life… Opposition
towards company.

CAIUS (*as before, to Lupu*): Do you have the sensation of insects crawling
over your skin?

LUPU (*thinking, so as to answer correctly*): No. (*Two seconds later, he adds by
way of explanation*): Under the skin.

KIRILL (*as before, continuing his examination*): … Aberrant interpretations
of reality.

CAIUS (*likewise*): … Frequent in paranoid schizophrenia, psychoses of
involution.

(George assiduously assists in the consultation. On three occasions he too attempts to express his observations in psychiatric jargon, but each time, as he pulls his bunched-up handkerchief out of his mouth, he realises, astounded, that absolutely nothing suitable comes into his head. He can barely refrain from the urge to swear. The fourth time he opens his mouth he manages at last to get into the verbal groove of the consultation.)

GEORGE *(curtly asks the patient, unable to refrain also from winking at him)*: Do you feel like a wolf?

(Waldo emerges from the fourth tent, at the back of the stage, and heads towards Lupu's bed. On the fourth tent is written the word "HEAVEN". Waldo is dressed soberly and luxuriously. The same story: underneath, the pyjamas, which in his case are better looked after; and on top, few items, but among the most precious to be found in the ward. Over his hospital garb he wears the gold and silver-stitched stole of the Orthodox priest. At his waist, he wears the imam's dagger. On his head sits a ring, part of some medical instrument, made of a strip of steel, which now resembles a crown and confers on him a majestic appearance.
Waldo comes to a halt by Lupu's pillow, in the middle of the suite of "governors". Everyone in the ward is strongly influenced by the presence of Waldo. Waldo makes a short ocular examination of Lupu.)

CAIUS *(hands a sheet of paper to Waldo)*: The medical chart.

WALDO *(intent on Lupu, then the chart, then Lupu again)*: Laseque, a martyred medical expert, postulated… *(A fleeting glance at Marcel.)* That the distance between illusion and hallucination is the same as the distance between gossip and slander.

(Both the "governors" and the six patients scattered among the beds – whom we shall name for the sake of expediency the "subjects" – cease all other activity. Waldo's every word and gesture reverberate.)

WALDO *(referring to the bites Lupu has given the Prince)*: The patient reacts with an aggression that might result in medical and legal implications.

(The listeners react in the same way. Asymptotic increase in agitation.)

WALDO (*the moment he makes the decision*): He requires tranquilisers.
(*Well-restrained nervous release and relaxation on the part of the listeners.*)
A prescription of Neutropitrill, an incisive neuroleptic, marked anti-
depressive valences, useful in combating obsessive-compulsive impulses.
To be administered at the normal dosage for twenty-one consecutive days.

(*George rummages and pulls the Netropitrill out of a little bag of medicaments, a
stock partly made up of flacons discovered in cupboards around the ward, partly of
pills not swallowed by the patients and hoarded over time. George shakes two pills
into his palm. He thrusts them into Lupu's mouth. Caius makes him drink some
water from a chamber pot he wears slung over his shoulder. Kirill checks Lupu's
open mouth. He inserts his finger to check whether Lupu has really swallowed the
pills or if he is hiding them under his tongue. Lupu is overwhelmed by a cloud
of joy at having got off so lightly. His state suddenly improves, seeming to be an
instantaneous and almost miraculous effect of the two pills.*)

WALDO (*to Lupu*): On your knees, will you cross yourself and declare that
your soul obeys only Holy Psychiatry?

(*Lupu slides out of bed. He gets down on all fours, his characteristic position. He
ceremoniously kisses Waldo's hand. He confirms – why not? – nodding his head.*)

LUPU: I do declare.

(*Then, when he is given to understand that he is free to go, Lupu scampers away,
whining happily around the ward.*
    *The group of examiners navigate slightly to the right, arriving by the Prince's
bedside. Capriciously, Waldo makes a negative sign. The group therefore continues
its migration to Zoli's bed and, Waldo having discreetly given his permission, the
four surround this patient.*
    *The same kind of consultation that has taken place with Lupu now unfolds for
Zoli. The "governors" perform the same well-known "dance". Waldo supervises,
standing to one side. Sheer terror rises even in the imperturbable Zoli.*)

KIRILL (*consultation*): Oligophrenia, state of psychical retardation….
Affecting all the mental processes.

CAIUS (*consultation*): Thickened integuments. Bruised colour. "Full-moon" face…

KIRILL (*likewise*): Cortical atrophy, sclerosis, cerebral lesions… Given training, a possibility – albeit reduced – of obtaining some conditioned reflexes.

CAIUS (*as before*): Flattened nose. Hypertrophied tongue. Thickened voice. Voluminous, "frog-like" abdomen…

GEORGE (*the handkerchief, to Zoli*): I'll show you how alcoholism breaks out strongly in the month of… (*and because he can no longer remember in which period, he concludes by adding a swearword*) … my arse.

KIRILL (*likewise*): Difficulty… in making abstractions and predicting phenomena…

WALDO (*examines the long roll of paper Caius has handed him*): The electroencephalogram looks catastrophic.

(*The "governors" cease the consultation and half turn towards Waldo.*)

WALDO: A congenital defect… (*The moment of decision*): The treatment is surgery.

(*With a murmur of approval, the "governors" rush upon Zoli, this time intending to bind him and immobilise him like a calf. In visceral terror and with all his might, Zoli struggles and screams. With jerky, efficient movements, the "governors" collaborate as follows: Kirill clambers on top of Zoli's chest, holding down his torso, arms and, partially, head; Caius also targets his head; George pulls two long nails from the bag of medicaments. George hammers the first nail into the top of Zoli's head, positioning it slightly to the left, using the mallet for testing reflexes. Then they swap roles. George takes his turn to immobilise Zoli's head, and Caius continues the surgical treatment, hammering the second nail into the top of Zoli's head, but more to the right.*
  A minute later, as suddenly as they had immobilised him, George, Caius and Kirill withdraw, releasing Zoli. The patient remains for a couple of seconds in bed,

suspecting that he is dead. Then, shuddering, Zoli sits up, leaps to his feet, amazed at being capable of moving and once he has ascertained that he can, he dances for joy at not being dead. The nails were probably positioned in two therapeutically well-chosen spots, because he feels better. The two nails in his head make Zoli look as though he has two antennae.)

WALDO (to Zoli, who continues to perform comical movements): Do you worship and believe only in Holy Psychiatry?

ZOLI (falls to his knees and kisses Waldo's hand. The first word he utters sounds distorted, because he is addressing Waldo freely and intentionally): Wo-o-or-ship! ... (*But then he reels off one of the sentences he seems to have learned by heart*): And miraculous cures occur whenever medical experts aerate the negative pressure that accumulates in your brain.

(Waldo's attention is diverted from the six patients who, since the beginning of Act Three, have more or less remained in their beds. The "subjects" realise this, come out of the paralysis with which they have followed the previous consultations, and recommence their usual, disordered activities, nonetheless taking care not to let the actions in which Waldo is about to engage out of their sight.

Waldo, accompanied by his guard, made up of the "governors", heads towards tent number two, upon which is pinned a piece of paper that reads "PRISON". George and Caius part the sheet as though they were drawing some curtains.

In the tent, alive and imprisoned, are Amanda, Paranasius and Zaid. Amanda, suspended in a harness, dangles from a rope two metres from the floor, slowly spinning and swaying. Paranaius has been thrust inside the cauldron full of dirty sheets. Zaid is sequestered in the middle of the huge metal box, in which the dirty dishes, spoons and solidified leftovers are deposited.

All three religious teachers are bound hand and foot, in such a way that it is impossible for them to escape from their place of incarceration. They are dressed partly in the clothes they wore at the start, namely those that have not been stolen. Even imprisoned, robbed and filthy, they have preserved their imposing and dignified attitudes.)

WALDO: Leave off the praying, meditation and good works, your holinesses, for the hour has come! (*To his suite of "governors"*): Release the three, my dears, for they will now go head to head in the tournament of religions.

(The "governors" remove the religious teachers from the places where they are held captive. They manhandle them like bales. They unbind them. They oblige them to move to their new places.)

WALDO (*to Caius, who has become a kind of secretary*): Give me the schedule.

CAIUS (*handing him a piece of paper*): Here you are.

WALDO: So, in the first semi-final, his holiness Paranasius and his holiness Ignatius were signed up to measure their powers against each other. But, surprise! (*To Paranasius*): Because Ignatius abandoned the match, you beat him 3-0, and because of his failure to turn up you qualified for the final, isn't that right, Underbelly of Hell?

PARANASIUS: I shall defend my ancestral faith whatever the circumstances… I could have beaten the papist weakling one-handed, Ball of Devils.

CAIUS (*speaking in his usual "oblique" manner, which is to say, not taking into account the impossibility of Ignatius competing any more*): We shall see.

GEORGE (*the handkerchief; taking up the strange eventuality contained in what Caius has said*): I'll dig him up, sit him on the chair and move his jaw up and down, as though he was arguing with the other ox.

WALDO: And in the second semi-final, battling for the honour of facing Paranasius in the final, his holiness Zaid will go head to head with his holiness Amanda.

AMANDA (*with his constant serenity, to Waldo*): If you want to call me "your holiness"…

KIRILL (*continuing, in derision, what he is certain Amanda was about to say*): But if you don't want to, don't tell me!

WALDO (*points to the centre of the ward*): The match will unfold right now and right here. They will be playing by the rules of the Marchioness.

OLYMPIA: Three questions posed regarding the religion of your opponent. The question, the adversary's answer, and the comments of the person posing the question as regards the adversary's answer. Each exchange shall not exceed more than a minute. First one asks a question, then the other... I have the stopwatch.

CAIUS (holding the pieces of paper with the rules; enquiring so that he can complete them): Are we also playing for third and fourth place?

WALDO: Ask their holinesses whether a religion has ever fought for third or fourth place.

(The three religious servants have been freed and, in the meantime, stretched their numb limbs.

Zaid and Amanda are in the middle of the stage. They are seated at a distance of two metres and facing each other. Face to face, but only in three-quarters view, so that both can also look at the audience and at the same time not have their backs completely turned to those seated at the large table on the stage. Zaid and Amanda have both received a stool, but have chosen to sit cross-legged on the floor. Looking from the audience, Zaid is on the left, and Amanda on the right.

At the large table, at which the four religious servants had been sitting in Act Two, Goerge, Caius, Waldo and Kirill are now seated. Paranasius is sitting on a chair to one side. He is separate from the six patients, the "subjects", who, out of curiosity, have also moved closer, forming a broad semicircle at the centre of which are Zaid and Amanda.)

WALDO (from the table, toying with the stopwatch): You put the first question, your holiness, Amanda.

AMANDA: ... I would ask my brother, if there is no objection, what has he understood from the teaching of Buddha?

WALDO: No, ask him a real question! A question about his Islamic religion.

ZAID (answering Amanda): That you are not worthy to be my brother and that it is an infidel doctrine. That is what I have understood.

AMANDA (*ponders, in order to find a question as suited as possible to Waldo's command, then he addresses Zaid*): You say that the entire universe is subject to a powerful and all-encompassing law which you name the law of Allah. You say that all things obey the law of Allah, and, for this reason, the whole world is bound to the Islamic religion. And that, in a certain sense, both he who worships other gods and he who worships no gods are still Muslims… I ask you: am I a Muslim?

MARCEL (*not pausing in his knitting, he casts a mistrustful glance at Amanda*): Maybe you are.

GEORGE (*to Zaid*): Listen, you hobbler, if you sleep with a Muslim woman don't you become a Muslim?

WALDO (*also to Zaid, referring to the question posed by Amanda*): Answer him.

ZAID: The earth rotates according to a pre-established law. From tiny electrons to huge galaxies, all things unfold, with great strictness, according to the laws ordained for them. (*Addressing Amanda in particular*): All your internal organs function according to the laws implanted in them. Islam means the submission of the entire universe to the will of Allah! … Because everything that exists in the world is subject to the will of Allah, it is possible to say that everything is Muslim. You are a "Muslim", whether you know it or not, whether you deny Allah or not, because you are subject to the divine will.

WALDO (*checking the stopwatch; to Zaid*): You have another fifteen seconds.

ZAID (*to Amanda*): In this sense, yes, you are a Muslim.

WALDO (*waits for the remaining seconds of the regulation minute to elapse; to Zaid*): Time's up. (*He addresses Amanda and once again starts the stopwatch.*) You may now comment on the answer to the question you posed.

AMANDA: There is no other commentary except the evidence that I am not a Muslim.

WALDO (*to Zaid, after starting the stopwatch again*): Now you may pose your first question regarding the Buddhist religion.

ZAID (*fidgets, thinking about what to ask; he decides; he addresses Amanda*): You teach people that the soul does not exist…

AMANDA (*amiably*): Yes. It has no real existence.

ZAID: If, according to your own teachings, the soul does not exist, and, if nothing that a man forms in this life passes into his next life, how can you lie that reincarnation exists? And how can you deceive, asserting that a man is weighed down by the non-fulfilments he has accumulated in his previous lives?

AMANDA (*to Zaid*): The one you do not wish to name your brother does not lie. And to the one whom you scorn it is forbidden to deceive. Just as a shepherd leads his sheep to pasture, old age and death lead the lives of men from one existence into another. What we reap today we have sown yesterday. And what we shall reap tomorrow is what we sow today. There are twelve interlinked causes that cause reincarnation.

WALDO (*the stopwatch*): You have another twelve seconds.

AMANDA: The thirst for life, attachment to things, and ignorance regarding the illusory character of the world are the main causes that produce reincarnation.

PICA (*tormented by a feeling of hunger, which is heightened by hearing the word in question*): Don't keep saying reincarnivorous!

WALDO (*to Amanda, referring to the time*): You're inside. (*To Zaid*): Commentary.

ZAID: The only cause that has ever produced any reincarnation is the lie sown by this scoundrel.

WALDO: The second set of questions. (*Addressing Amanda in sporting terms*): You have the first serve.

AMANDA (addressing Zaid): You say that all men's thoughts and deeds are decided by Allah in advance of them taking place... If the result of our discussion is pre-established what point is there in holding the discussion? If Allah has already decided that you shall win, why is there so little zeal in your face? And if Allah has decided that you shall lose, against whom do you act with zeal? ... Do you fight against Allah?

LUPU (to Zaid): Ow-oo! ... You're fighting against Allah, either you're a crusader and a Christian...

PICA (also to Zaid): Or... (*He doesn't know what else to say.*)

THE PRINCE: A Hindu... A friend of mine, a maharajah... (*He is interrupted and loses his train of thought. The beginning of his story interests no one and inspires trust in no one.*)

MARCEL (also takes part, just as easily influenced, in the self-goading of the entire group of "subjects" against Zaid): Have you seen Allah, because he doesn't come around here much... Because, otherwise, he'd wallop you in the head, he'd make mincemeat out of you!

ZAID (he rolls his eyes, full of feelings of scorn and rage against them all. He controls himself. He speaks plainly and, from habit, feels the place where his dagger used to hang from his girdle): The madness of the infidel hides beneath a tangle of words, but raises only dust and dead leaves... Praise be to Allah, who alone imparts life, wisdom, power, wealth and honour! All good things are in the hands of Allah, he represents them as he wishes and in proportions known only unto him. Of course, I do not know what Allah has deigned to decide as regards our confrontation. But the duty of every good Muslim is to act...

WALDO (following the stopwatch): You have another fifteen seconds to act.

ZAID (continuing): ... with honour and perseverance. Waiting to see whether Allah, praised be his name, has willed it to happen in one way or another.

WALDO (referring to the minute allotted to Zaid): Expired! (*To Amanda*): Commentary.

AMANDA: I have no comments to make.

KIRILL (from his place at the table, next to Waldo): It's damaging to the health not to have any comments to make.

MARCEL (referring, evidently, to what befell Ignatius): The baldy one has started tinkering with the time.

AMANDA: My comment is that predestination is due solely to Karma…

WALDO: No. Your minute for commentary has vanished. (*To Zaid, making a sign for him to put his question to Amanda*): Now it's your serve.

ZAID (to Amanda): The infidels were not content merely with the madness preached by Buddha, but they also transformed Buddhism into a cult dedicated to Buddha himself. The things he left behind became holy relics. Your illumination resides in the fact that you bow down and pray to the rotten tooth of a man in a place called… Kandy, I think it is. Tell me if I am wrong… Or you pray to the footprints left by Buddha. To statues and paintings depicting him…

WALDO: Fifteen seconds.

ZAID: … depicting Buddha. Is this not the basest and most complete idolatry?

MARCEL (to Amanda): You didn't say that you pray to a tooth…

RAPHAEL: Or maybe you pray that the pain won't give you a toothache.

THE PRINCE (also to Amanda): But, in this case, you wouldn't be Buddhists any longer, but dentists.

AMANDA (answering Zaid): The gods are not released from desires.

They are therefore subject to rebirth… But not even an army of all the attractions on Earth could bring Buddha back into the world. In depictions, Buddha is shown smiling. The smile does not mean profane serenity. His smile signifies the spiritual joy of the one who has discovered illumination. This spiritualised joy is the very state of penetrating to Final Extinction.

GEORGE (with satisfaction): Nirvana… That is, the happier you are, the more that happiness makes you snuff it.

ZAID (to Amanda): Is this or is this not idolatry?

AMANDA: It is not idolatry. We do not worship a rotten tooth.

WALDO (to Amanda): And the minute has elapsed. (*To Zaid*): Commentary.

ZAID: Both the infidel and the tooth are rotten.

WALDO (to Amanda): It is your turn once again, your holiness. But serve him one that will smash his teeth out, because it's your last question.

AMANDA (to Zaid): Why do you consider that I, brother Ignatius and any man of any religion other than Islam must necessarily pay you tribute?

ZAID (to Amanda): This is a new lie, that you must necessarily pay me tribute… Do you wish to convert to Islam?

AMANDA (politely but firmly): No.

ZAID (to Amanda): In his profound wisdom, Mohammed, the seal of prophets, taught us that before any man of another faith, which is to say an infidel, there lie three paths: either he transform himself into a subject of the true faith, which you have stubbornly refused to do; or else he should pay a tax; or else he should become a slave, but I don't think that you, even as a slave, would be of any use to anybody.

WALDO (to Zaid): Fifteen seconds.

ZAID (to Amanda): And so better you pay your tribute.

WALDO (to Amanda): Commentary.

GEORGE (the handkerchief; he derisively imitates Amanda): I have no comments to make.

AMANDA: It is unjust to impose the payment of tribute… And for those who have already paid it, such as brother Ignatius, the fact did indeed prove damaging to the health.

CAIUS: The baldy one is tinkering like mad with the time.

WALDO (making an effort not to refer too much to what Amanda has said): As you wish. *(Addressing them all, and Zaid in particular)*: And so here we are. There now follows the formulation of the last question of the semi-final.

ZAID (inclines the upper part of his torso towards Amanda and speaks to him with a lack of harshness hitherto unseen): Monk, answer me straight… What do you, the Buddhists, believe: Does God exist?

PICA (in consternation): How could He not? Otherwise what are we all doing here?

AMANDA (to Zaid): Buddha concentrated only on the problem of man's salvation. And as he discovered that man can save himself by his own powers, he was no longer interested in the problem of the existence of God.

MARCEL: Aha!

AMANDA: "Try to distinguish the things unnecessary to salvation, in order not to fall into the most perilous errors…" What is the trap from which Buddha saved us? …By not allowing the problem of the existence of God, he eliminated the most serious cause of misunderstandings between men.

ZAID (to Amanda): Answer me directly. What do you believe? Does God exist? Or does God not exist?

THE PRINCE (imitating the kind of answer Amanda is wont to give): If you wish, then God exists…

LUPU: …But if you do not wish, then God does not exist.

WALDO (the stopwatch): Fifteen seconds.

AMANDA (with the same unshakable serenity, to Zaid): I don't know. Maybe. He does not exist.

WALDO (the stopwatch): …The minute is up. (*To Zaid*): Commentary.

ZAID: The teaching of this piece of filth says: I do not believe that Allah exists purely so that I can pray to my own backside. Because it, my backside, will save me.

MARCEL: Really? Is that what he teaches will save us? His bottom?

THE PRINCE: No. He teaches us that each of us prays to our own backside. And that our backsides will save us separately.

GEORGE (the handkerchief; he addresses his own backside): O bottom, if you are really my servant. Quick march, fetch me two kilos of alcohol! (*He waits a few seconds, during which time he himself is curious to see what will happen. Then, reaching a conclusion, to Amanda*): It's not fetching it…

WALDO: And with that the grand phase of the semi-finals of the world religions championship draw to a close! …The results will be communicated to you shortly.

(*On hearing Waldo's words, George, Caius and Kirill, deploying according to a pre-established plan, rise from the jury table and, with the demeanour of medical staff, head towards the two religious servants in the middle of the ward.*
    Zaid and Amanda, who up to now have confronted each other sitting

cross-legged on the floor, now also rise, but remain in the same place. George, Caius and Kirill walk around them in a circle once. Then they spread out around Zaid, circling him for a time and examining him, preoccupied. All of a sudden, the "governors" finish with Zaid and go on to examine Amanda, according to the same pattern: they surround him silently, circle him, and inspect him closely. While they are undertaking these manoeuvres, George, Caius and Kirill cast glances at Waldo, seeking his approval. Waldo remains seated alone at the long table, from where, in his turn, he watches motionlessly the three "governors".

When George, Caius and Kirill circle Amanda for the third time, and cast an interrogative glance in the direction of the table, Waldo at last gives the agreed signal. He nods once, granting them permission and urging them to act. George, Caius and Kirill now close the circle around Amanda and subject him to a kind of medical consultation.)

GEORGE (*the handkerchief; to Amanda*): Do you know what Holy Psychiatry says about you?

KIRILL (*speaks impersonally, using the same air with which scientific truths are uttered, while he carries out the consultation of Amanda*): Primitive thinking… Operates by error… Mystic temperament… Drives away reason, taking refuge either in loss of identity or hallucinatory states of delusion…

CAIUS (*takes part in the consultation with the greatest concentration; in addition, from time to time, he jots down notes on pieces of paper*): A choice between reality and fiction, in favour of fiction… Impervious to the objective proofs of reason…

KIRILL (*as before*): …Contiguous with schizophrenia, in the obsessive neurosis and regressive psychical processes.

CAIUS (*in the same way, but pausing to question Amanda*): Are you aiming at a gradual purification of the soul and at the loss of the 'I' in impersonal transcendence?

AMANDA (*impenetrable and polite*): If you wish to express yourself in this way… Yes.

CAIUS (*as before; resuming his medical observations and no longer addressing Amanda directly*): Morbid alteration of the truth… Construction of imaginary events… Manifestations whereby he strives to gain the attention and esteem of those around him.

(*At the same time, Waldo also rises from the table and approaches the three who are examining Amanda. As Waldo approaches Amanda, the interest of the entire ward is awakened. Continuing to surround the Buddhist monk, George, Caius, and Kirill arrange themselves in such a way as to allow Waldo to come face to face with Amanda. Waldo stops five feet away from Amanda, and stands calmly with his hands behind his back.*)

CAIUS (*hands Waldo a roll of paper*): Here is an older electroencephalogram. (*He points to Amanda*): When Olympia caught hold of him by mistake and took him away with the whole lot of us for tests.

(*Waldo takes the piece of paper, examines it quickly, and hands it back to Caius, with an air that suggests it would be better if Caius himself interpreted it. Waldo behaves as though he had more important business. His more important business is silently, piercingly to look Amanda straight in the eye.*)

CAIUS (*he takes back the roll of paper handed to him by Waldo, examines it carefully, and analyses it in the same medical tone as before*): The electroencephalogram dated… Captures the patient in an ecstatic state… The diffuse rhythm of the alpha waves… Shows detachment from the real world…

KIRILL (*receives the electroencephalogram from Caius, examines it, and interprets it in his turn, using the same medical tone*): …Classic patterns for those suffering chronic delirium… Extremely dangerous… Because of their redoubtable power of conviction… They can unleash, at any time, destructive bursts of collective psychosis.

(*Meanwhile, the nervous tension in the ward increases, because of the intensity with which Waldo continues to stare Amanda in the eye.*)

WALDO (at last speaking, even very amiably, to Amanda): To take part in the world championship of religions without believing that God exists. Is exactly the same as using a skeleton key to enter at night the houses of some very nice people and trying to kill them... (*He places his left hand on Amanda's shoulder.*) Why, my friend, did you enter the show without a ticket?

CAIUS (allows a few seconds to elapse in order for the menace that has accumulated in the air to be felt by all. Then to Waldo): The treatment!

RAPHAEL: Pretty please, Waldo. Let it be a medicamenticial one.

PICA: Give him a bed and let him go dizzy with hunger. Until he gets better.

GEORGE (the handkerchief; he comes insolently close to Amanda): You've got a face that's twice as stupid as my bottom's!

KIRILL (also to Amanda): What a wormy apple skin has grown over your pate!

AMANDA (unflinchingly calm and serene): "...Just as the elephant endures, in battle, the arrows shot by bows. So I endure the insults flung by unworthy men."

KIRILL: How strange! ...You have nothing holy and yet it is us, the unworthy, who are going to make you better!

WALDO (solemnly, to Amanda): Do you agree to worship and to serve, and for your whole fate to depend only on Holy Psychiatry?

AMANDA (to Waldo): Even if you wish it, I do not agree...

(*While Amanda and Waldo are speaking, Kirill discreetly breaks away from the group, and removes three iron crowbars from a hiding place behind one of the filing cabinets. He fetches them in his arms, and distributes one each to George and Caius, keeping the third for himself.*)

AMANDA (still to Waldo): ...And however much force might insist, I am still against.

WALDO: Impressive... (*He is talking to Amanda, but looking at the three "governors", who have regrouped behind the Buddhist monk.*) Then what I recommend for you is musical therapy... (*He makes sure his acolytes have armed themselves.*) The fanfare! ... (*And because the "governors" do not understand, he explains to them, by an imperceptible, but eloquent gesture, the way in which he orders them to proceed.*) Let us hear you bang the big bass drum! (*Instantly understanding Waldo's order, the three, George, Caius and Kirill begin to bang the "big bass drum" with their crowbars. This is none other than the shaven skull of Amanda. At the very first blow, Amanda falls.*

Bending over him, the three continue to hit his head with the crowbars, rhythmically, exactly as though it were a drum. Moreover, puffing out their cheeks, they also use their mouths to imitate the noise of a drum: boom, boom-boom-boom, boom-boom! ...Amanda is slain. His head is smashed and bloody.)

WALDO: And behold, after sixty-seven previous unsuccessful existences, animal, human, and other, only Holy Psychiatry has been able to make his holiness Amanda better, freeing him from the chains of Karma and placing him in the Final Extinction!

GEORGE (as a sign of agreement, he kicks Amanda's corpse in the ribs): Stick it up my nirvana!

KIRILL (together with George and Caius, drags the fresh corpse over to the square of floor that belongs to tent number one, the one whose sheet has the word "CEMETERY" written on it): Let's leave... the carrion unburied... for a while, as proof that it will be disincarnated, not reincarnated!

PICA (although he continues to mangle words and sentences, has the courage to declare himself decidedly against this crime. He addresses the entire group of killers, George, Caius, and Walso): Either with carnations. Or without carnations... It's no good what you're doing!

MARCEL (tends to his rag baby. Then resumes his knitting. He addresses only

Waldo): That Olympia's really going to break her broom handle over your back when she hears about Holy Psychiatry!

WALDO (*gives the order, evenly, showing he is entirely indifferent to the remarks of Pica and Marcel*): Those faithful to Holy Psychiatry must not sit together with those not faithful to Holy Psychiatry.

(*Waldo goes and takes his place on the bench below the window, sitting at the long table and keeping watch on the rest of the ward.*

Carrying out Waldo's orders, the "governors" make changes in the room. They separate those regarded as faithful to Holy Psychiatry – Lupu and Zoli – from the other four members of the "subjects".

The action unfolds as follows: first, George, Caius and Kirill pick up the metal beds of Lupu and Zoli and move them alongside tent number three, the "GOVERNMENT". They leave the beds outside the tent, orienting them parallel to the wall at the back of the stage, so as to occupy as little space as possible at the centre of the ward. Then, George, Caius and Kirill move closer together the beds of Marcel, Pica, the Prince and Raphael, which had been left at an exaggerated distance apart after the removal of the other two beds. Finally, the "governors" grab Lupu and Zoli and give them a fresh dose of the treatment they have been prescribed by Waldo, in the name of Holy Psychiatry. They force Lupu to swallow another two pills. They make him drink some water. They thrust their fingers once more into his mouth to check whether he has swallowed the pills. They are about to hammer more nails into Zoli's head. But in the end they decide not to. They have fun pulling the two nails already implanted. They push the nails deeper into his brain.

Then George, Caius and Kirill place Zoli on all fours, like Lupu. They tie a special leash around Zoli's and Lupu's necks. The leashes have a noose at one end, which can be tightened around the neck, thereby choking the wearer. At the other end, the rope of the leash is held by George. For a good while, George will walk around the room as though tethered to Zoli and Lupu, who will advance like two dogs. Now and then, George whacks them with the handkerchief he keeps in his mouth.)

GEORGE (*holding Lupu and Zoli in the leash*): Bad people spoil... good people. (*He kicks Zoli, goading him to insult his former fellows in the group of "subjects", i.e. Marcel, Pica, the Prince, and Raphael. The four, Marcel, Pica, the*

Prince and Raphael now make up a new group, which, for expediency, we shall call the "unaligned group" or the "unaligned"): Tell them how shitty they are!

ZOLI (his behaviour has altered. He reacts more to what is going on around him. Out of fear, he tries to please the ones who give him orders. Although very cloudy, his speech, still consisting of residual phrases, begins to have a different connexion to reality. For example, at this moment, he utters his phrase looking in the direction of the four members of the "unaligned group"): The mental cartilage… which covers the brain. Is enflamed, when you cannot manage to avoid… bad company.

GEORGE (pleasantly surprised by Zoli's answer, bends down and plays with him, as though he were a little dog): Good dog! Good little doggy! Maybe I'll send you out to fetch me some brandy sometime.

WALDO: Look at Paranasius, you'd think he was dribbling a football, ready to shoot at the goal! …Are you ready to recommence the Championship, Devils' Delight?

PARANASIUS: The worms, father. The worms will be smacking their lips in delight, when they feast on your carrion! …Ready to give the Islamic Satan the right and left.

WALDO: Ready for action, Zaid?

ZAID (to Waldo, referring to Paranasius): Football you said. If you do not convert, I will chop off your head and let the dogs play football with it.

(George yanks the leashes to which are tied Zoli and Lupu, whom he regards as "his dogs", so as to prove that he will not allow them to play football, as others might like. Zoli and Lupu whimper like dogs.
A few moments of silence.
Caius looks interrogatively at Waldo. Waldo gazes at Caius, first of all motionless. Then, slightly moving his head, he gives Caius his tacitly requested permission. Yes, he seems to tell Caius. Now is good. You can do the thing you asked me whether I allowed you to do.)

CAIUS (*gets ready to make an announcement. He goes to the middle of the room and begins, in a resounding voice*): …Ladies and gentlemen! … (*He stops, asking Waldo in a lower voice*): Can I say "ladies" as well?

WALDO (*smiling*): Ask Marcel.

CAIUS (*turns to Marcel to ask him, but doesn't manage to open his mouth*): …

MARCEL (*to Caius*): I'm not Waldo's father. And Waldo's not my daughter… But he won't get too annoyed if you say "ladies" too.

CAIUS (*resuming his announcement*): Gentlemen, what is about to commence is not merely a great event, but the event up to which the history of the world has been leading! Whether you are a Jew, an Aztec, a schismatic, or a Hindu, roll up to discover which of the religions will win, and by converting to that religion, all your wishes will be fulfilled! Soon we will know the only true religion in the world… Watch the final of the World Championship of Religions! …

(*Zaid and Paranasius take up their places at the centre of the ward ready for the contest. Zaid is at a point farther from the jury table, Paranasius closer.*

Kirill approaches Zaid and Paranasius, ready for the toss. First of all, to see which places they will occupy, according to the rules. Secondly, to decide in which order they will ask each other questions.

Kirill takes out the coin for the toss and shows it to Zaid and Paranasius so that they can inspect it. They inspect it.

The four from the "unaligned group", Marcel, Pica, the Prince and Raphael, get down from their beds, and once more fan out in a semicircle, ready to watch the final between Zaid and Paranasius.)

KIRILL (*places the coin on his thumbnail, ready to flick it spinning into the air. He signals for Zaid to call heads or tails exactly at the moment the coin is spinning in the air.*)

ZAID (*choosing just in time*): Heads.

PARANASIUS: Money is the eye of the devil…

KIRILL (*dextrously catches the coin in his palm and reveals which side is facing up. He shows them both the coin. To Zaid*): You win.

ZAID (*opting for his terrain*): I remain where I am.

KIRILL (*is ready to repeat the toss. This time, he invites Paranasius to call. To Paranasius*): For kick off. (*He flicks the coin up in the air once more.*)

PARANASIUS (*he chooses at the last moment*): Tails.

KIRILL (*catches the coin and checks on which side it has fallen up. He shows both of them. The side facing up is, indeed, tails. To Paranasius*): You kick off, your holiness.

(*Zaid and Paranasius remain in the places they have chosen, this time according to the rules and after the toss. They ready themselves for the confrontation. They puff up their chests. They adopt bellicose postures. They bore each other with their eyes. In order not to place himself in a position that might seem inferior, Zaid does not sit cross-legged on the floor. Zaid and Paranasius are ready for battle and standing up.*)

WALDO (*from the jury table, giving the contestants their final instructions*): Marchioness Olympia's rules. (*To Paranasius*): You place it on the ground and kick off quickly. (*He sets his stopwatch. Also to Paranasius, giving the signal for the final to commence*): First question!

(*Caius and Kirill are also seated, to the right and left of Waldo, at the jury table. George continues to walk around the ward, holding his two "dogs", Zoli and Lupu, on the leash, stopping them when he wants them to go around the "unaligned" or the finalists.*
    Waldo starts his stopwatch.)

PARANASIUS (*solemn. Fervent. To Zaid*): …I want you to swear before

God! …Is the Son of God and the Saviour of the Christians – Jesus Christ – a Muslim?

ZAID (with the same fiery fervour. Not allowing himself to be in the least bit intimidated by Paranasius. On the contrary, striving to dominate and instil terror in the Orthodox): The question was put incorrectly. I shall answer only the good part of it. Of course, Jesus is a Muslim.

PARANASIUS (raises his left hand to his heart. Then gathers his strength): Is Jesus Christ, the son of the living God and revelation of all Christian truths, a Muslim?

ZAID: He is. You too might follow his example.

PARANASIUS: I call upon you for the third time. Flee from the fires of hell above which you sit! …A Muslim?

(George makes a sign to Waldo, showing him that Paranasius has broken the "Marchioness Olympia's" rules, by putting too many questions at once.

Waldo answers George by another sign, communicating that he, Waldo, knows what to do.)

ZAID: Before the coming of Mohammed, the greatest of the prophets sent by Allah there was Jesus, son of Mary.

PARANASIUS (choking with indignation): Jesus Christ was sent by Allah?

WALDO (keeping a close eye on the stopwatch, addresses Paranasius and Zaid): Your minutes for question and answer are at a close. (*Then he addresses Paranasius alone*): There now follows your minute for commentary on his answer.

PARANASIUS (to Zaid, barely restraining himself from striking him): You speak a language instilled in you by Satan when he kisses you on the mouth! … (*To all those in the ward, apart from Zaid*): Believe, O my sons, that God is the Father, the Son, which is to say Jesus Christ, and the

Holy Spirit! Threefold according to His image. Nonetheless one God according to his being… Just as the globe of the sun, the sunbeam, and the light, although three, are nevertheless a single sun… (*Turning around and addressing only Zaid once more*): And you – may you be cursed throughout the ages for the way in which you utter the most diabolical filth, with an insolence as though you were narrating your choicest deeds!

KIRILL (*summarising, in football terms, the state of play between Paranasius and Zaid at this moment*): His holiness (*he gestures to show he is referring to Paranasius*) has taken three shots at the goal. And his right-believingness (*with another gesture he shows he is referring to Zaid*) has made three saves, with a punch, a header, and a kick… After that, his holiness went pale once again, and the ball hit the goalpost, which you can hear thrumming even now! …

MARCEL (*captivated by the unfolding match, he enters the discussion, giving Zaid some sporting advice*): Now you ask, ugly!

(*A few seconds of silence. Zaid prepares to pose his question, Paranasius to respond.*)

ZAID: Jesus is the son of God?

PARANASIUS (*cautiously, all his senses keen, in order for him not to fall into some trap*): … With your own mouth you said it.

ZAID (*continuing the previous question*): Mary, the mother of Jesus, is "the mother of God"?

PARANASIUS (*with growing suspicion*): … Yes.

ZAID (*authoritatively, staring Paranasius straight in the eye*): Consume your entire minute with your answer!

PARANASIUS (*maintaining his gaze, but with extreme foresight*): … Let's see where you're leading up to.

(*Zaid and Paranasius are eyeing each other like two roosters. Paranasius falls silent, allowing the minute for his answer to elapse. As the minute is ending, the Orthodox priest intervenes tardily.*)

PARANASIUS (*confused, out of the corner of his mouth to Zaid*): Which question do you want me to answer?

(*Waldo gestures with the meaning that Paranasius' minute has indeed expired and that now he is inviting Zaid to use his minute for commentary on the Orthodox priest's answer.*)

ZAID (*to Paranasius*): It means that, in your religion, God the Father is married to Mary…

PARANASIUS (*a furious outburst directed at Zaid*): May you be accursed!

ZAID (*continuing, to Zaid*): …Because she could not have conceived Jesus out of wedlock… But all your books say that Mary was married to Joseph, the carpenter.

LUPU (*on all fours, with the leash held by George around his neck. From now on, he speaks above all to please George and his group*): Ow-ooo! Industrious woman!

GEORGE (*treating George like a hound dog*): Good dog! … (*He shows Zaid to Lupu*): Lick the simpleton!

(*Lupu and Zoli rush to lick the imam. Zaid makes as though to kick them. Lupu and Zoli withdraw, whimpering like two puppies.*)

MARCEL (*recalling the discovery made at the beginning of the First Act*): Vasilica. Vasilica is the Virgin Mary.

CAIUS (*addressing Paranasius and speaking once more in his aberrant, "oblique" way*): Yes. Didn't you teach us that Vasilica is married to God the Father?

ZAID (*taking up the thread of his commentary and trying not to let himself be disturbed by the illogical evolution of the reactions. He addresses Paranasius in the same tone of rage and condemnation*): Why do you darken the glory of Allah saying that he might have a son? And why do you dishonour him, with your invention that he might be married to a mortal, and one who is, at the same time, married to another??! …But Allah is solely Allah! …

WALDO (*to Zaid, consulting his stopwatch*): You have ten seconds left.

ZAID (*to Paranasius*): …And you, all those who have a filthy religion. In the flames of hell. We shall continually renew your skin, the better for you to taste the punishment!

(*Waldo makes a signal to Paranasius to utter the second of the three questions which he must, according to the rules, put to Zaid.*)

PARANASIUS (*to the entire assembly, but especially to the jury*): …I am going to provide proof, yet again, that this lickspittle… (*he is obviously referring to Zaid*) lies as easily as he breathes! (*To Zaid*): You speak of persons too lofty for you to be able to touch with your mind… And you say that they do things which you yourself reckon sinful: the marriage of a person with more than one other person at the same time… Therefore, it means that all those who worship Allah avoid such sickening deeds with the greatest horror. You avoid them, no? …Was Mahomet married with one woman or more than one woman?

(*Waldo confirms, by a gesture, that the minute reserved for the second question to be put by Paranasius has come to a close. Also mutely, Waldo shows Zaid that he will begin to time his minute from the moment he starts to answer the question of the Orthodox priest.*)

ZAID: …At the age of twenty-five, Mohammed – peace be upon him! Married a noble widow…

THE PRINCE: Vivat!

ZAID: …of forty, Khadija by name. In the beginning, she drove away Mohammed's doubts, she assured him that he was Allah's chosen one, she was his first follower. As long as Khadija lived, she was the prophet's only wife… In the Koran is contained concern for the widows and orphans of those who perish in war. The right-believer is permitted to take up to four wives.

MARCEL: Didn't I tell you?!

THE PRINCE: That's my kind of religion!

PICA (to Zaid): But do the wives know about each other?

(Disoriented and astonished, Zaid makes the mistake of interrupting his exposition to address Pica.)

ZAID: What do you mean, do they know?!

RAPHAEL (very polite and timid, performs for Pica approximately the same translation service he used to perform in the past, for Tanasîcu. To Zaid): He means, do they know he is faithful to each of them?

CAIUS ("obliquely", also to Zaid): After every war, are they allowed to take another fourteen or fifteen wives?

KIRILL (with VOICE NUMBER 2, the only voice he has used in this segment of the play, in the places where it is not otherwise specified): Zaid has four ugly hags he uses to frighten and chase away his believers during prayers. When he bequeathes you his wives, how are you going to cope, Marcel?

MARCEL (seriously, to Zaid): Your babies I'll take. The old women I won't.

ZAID (with an effort to control himself, resumes his exposition): …The wives are exempted from all business outside the home…

(Waldo makes a sign that the end of his minute is approaching.)

ZAID: …And just as it is true that Allah rules the heavens, earth and all they contain therein. So there is no happier situation for women than in Islam!

(*In general, the audience are more unconvinced than ever by this sermon of Zaid.*)

WALDO (*to Zaid*): And no place cooler for your feet than in the burning coals of hell… (*To Kirill, with reference to the most recent exposition by Zaid, considered to be inadequate*): Can't you smell singed flesh?

KIRILL (*with VOICE NUMBER 2*): It's sizzling… His holiness (*i.e. Paranasius, of course*) has come up the wing, he dodges two defenders and shoots, without much force, at the goal. But the right-believer (*it results that he is referring to Zaid*) still lets the ball through his legs… And indeed, now it does smell like something is roasting.

(*Waldo signals to Paranasius, for the Orthodox priest to make use of his minute's commentary on the answer given by Zaid.*)

PARANASIUS (*quick on the uptake, he gets the idea and starts talking about Zaid and those of the same faith as Zaid*): Both roasted and mendacious, as I have always demonstrated… Mahomet married thirteen women, after the death of his first wife! …Once, even with a little girl only nine years old! He calls happy the female slaves forced to mate in threes, in fours, worse than beasts.

GEORGE (*tries to get Zoli to mount Lupu, as though the two were mating like dogs*): That's not at all bad.

PARANASIUS (*fixes George with his gaze and continues with what he has to say*): But God commands that man should be the husband of a single woman… the two must be Orthodox. Love each other. Married by an Orthodox priest.

WALDO (*looking at his stopwatch. It is understood that the number he utters refers to the seconds remaining*): Ten…

KIRILL (*with VOICE NUMBER 2, proving that he knows in advance everything Paranasius is going to say*): And the purpose of marriage…

PARANASIUS: And the purpose of marriage is to give birth to children and to raise them in the holy traditions of the Orthodox Church.

(*Waldo wordlessly asks Zaid to put his second question to the Orthodox priest. As usual, Waldo has his stopwatch at the ready. He starts it.*)

ZAID (*heatedly, to Paranasius*): …The lie adorned with cunning leads to the punishment beyond which there is no other punishment… You say: "I love God. I am a Christian. I respect the holy books…" But the books, which were holy, you falsified them! You are not a Christian, because you do not truly know what Jesus taught! And you hate God, because His commandments, those left unfalsified, you read them only in order to find out how to behave exactly against them! …

PARANASIUS (*seething with indignation, to Zaid*): I hate God?!

GEORGE (*tugging at the leashes of Lupu and Zoli, addresses Paranasius, referring to Zaid*): Buy a dog from me, to bite him and kill the dolt.

PARANASIUS (*indignant*): I rebel against the divine commandments?!

GEORGE (*continuing to show off Lupu and Zoli as dogs. To Paranasius*): Give me two pints of communion wine. And these two will gnaw the bones of all those who've drunk, even only once, with Mahomet.

ZAID (*to Paranasius*): …Does it not say in your Bible that God is a spirit and forbids you, on pain of death, to worship images of any of his creations, be they man, animal or star?

(*Waldo makes his familiar gesture to signal that the minute allocated to Zaid for his question is almost at a close.*)

PARANASIUS (*haughty and relieved, as though by his answer to this question he has as good as won the contest*): It says it on almost every page.

ZAID (*continues. To Paranasius*): …Then why are your churches full of icons and idols, more than any pagan temple?

PARANASIUS (he cannot believe his ears): Idols in our churches?!

GEORGE (not giving up the idea of getting his hands on some alcohol by selling Zoli and Lupu as dogs. After having tried using nice words, he now attempts intimidation. To Paranasius): Haven't I seen you cramming them in with your foot, because there were so many you couldn't close the church door behind you?!

PICA (to Paranasius): And because there still wasn't enough room, you brought... *(he points to the large Orthodox icon and the smaller icons, strewn over the Orthodox priest's robes and alongside him)* ... those planks...

THE PRINCE (to Paranasius): ...Wounding my subjects...

MARCEL (to Paranasius): ...And forcing the children to wet themselves, out of fright at the ugly faces painted on them.

(Paranasius is dumbstruck by the insolence of this discussion of things reckoned by him to be of immense worth.

He sways. He gathers his strength. He returns to the theological fray. He is still shaken.)

PARANASIUS: From what I can hear, I have fallen to the bottom of hell...

MARCEL: I told you that was where you'd end up!

(Waldo silently warns Paranasius that his minute is slipping away.)

PARANASIUS (answering Zaid): There is no greater enmity than that between the Orthodox Church and idols. Idols are the image of false gods invented by the minds of men. Icons are the image of the true God.

RAPHAEL: How can you tell the difference?

PARANASIUS: Even by the holiness of their gazes!

PICA: What if the idols put on airs and try to gaze at you more holy like?

THE PRINCE (quite sincere): At that moment they are icons. But after that they turn back into false gods.

PARANASIUS (struggling not to let himself be affected by the comments of those around him): Orthodox icons are artistic representations of Jesus, the Mother of God or the saints. Often the holy icons receive the divine power to work miracles.

GEORGE (battling to make a deal. To Paranasius. With reference to the wine he has requested): Even if you bring me it not quite so blessed, I'll make these two (*he indicates Lupu and Zoli*) pray to them, nicer than you worship them.

PARANASIUS: I do not worship the holy icons!!

PICA: How's that?

PARANASIUS: It is a sin to worship the holy icons!

MARCEL: Then why do you teach your parishioners to kneel in front of them, to light candles, to kiss them all the time?!

PARANASIUS (with a sly air and delighted in the interest that has been aroused): Many see, few understand. (*To all those present, but especially to Zaid and the "unaligned group"*): Your eyes are obscured by the bonds of unbelief… (*Enlightening them, in a superior manner*): The true Christian does not worship icons, but in the presence of icons!

WALDO (to Paranasius): Fifteen seconds.

PARANASIUS: …Pure worship is not directed at wood and paint. But to the persons in Heaven whose image is painted on the icon!

WALDO (referring to Paranasius' minute for his answer): Expired… (*He addresses Zaid and begins to set his stopwatch for the commentary on the way in which the Orthodox priest has answered*): You.

ZAID: You have all heard the groans of the devil who tries to make white black and black white… They say that their idols and icons are merely ordinary things that help them to concentrate. But then, what is the difference between the worship savages accord their devil gods and the worship the Christians accord these ordinary things?! …Where God said: "No!" they nonetheless cast themselves into the most rabid idolatry! And what is more they alter the words of God in order to consider themselves saints when they make a mockery of the commandments…

KIRILL (with VOICE NUMBER 2): From outside the six-yard area?

CAIUS: From outside.

KIRILL (with VOICE NUMBER 2, to George): Chest control?

GEORGE (makes a negative gesture, i.e. no chest control of the ball): …

KIRILL (with VOICE NUMBER 2, summarising once again in football terms the latest confrontation): And so, from thirty-five metres. With the ball in mid-air. The right-believer (*makes a sign to show he is talking about Zaid*) makes a kick which not only clears the goal line but tears open the back of the net… And although his holiness (*indicates Paranasius*) is still pretending there hasn't been any goal. He is gradually getting used to the idea.

CAIUS (very formally. Makes an announcement): Ladies and gentlemen! This is how it is with people: each and every one of us feels as though, every ten minutes, he has been snatched away by a host of devils. Beaten until he vomits blood. Then put back unnoticed. And nevertheless, no one has the courage to talk about this feeling. Herein resides the success of religion! … Ladies and gentlemen! These holy gentlemen will put to each other one final question. We shall see which of them will be the victor and which of them will win the right to negotiate for us with the herds of devils…

LUPU (walking around on all fours and tugging at the leash held by George): Haven't you owoo heard him cursing?! …Paranasius has already established diplomatic communication with the devils.

THE PRINCE (*to Paranasius and Zaid; impartially*): Both of you are so ugly… That the devils invite you to dinner to scare the devil kiddies.

(*Waldo gestures to Paranasius indicating that it is time for him to utter his third question. Waldo starts the stopwatch.*)

PARANASIUS (*to Zaid*): I am going to pose you a question that will make the blood spurt out of your ears. With your own mouth you will condemn yourself. Your tongue has but to budge and you will slit your own throat… So, answer us this: did Jesus Christ, the one whom you say you love… did Jesus Christ, by His death on the Holy Cross, redeem you from your sins?

(*Waldo, with another gesture, orders Zaid to answer the question put by Paranasius. Waldo starts the stopwatch for Zaid's answer.*)

ZAID (*to Paranasius*): You talk as though Jesus had been crucified on some cross or other.

PARANASIUS (*thinking that Zaid has made some mistake in expressing himself and wishing to point it out*): Well, wasn't he?

ZAID (*to Paranasius, but, more than previously, also addressing the group of conspirators, especially Waldo*): Behold in how few words how many lies a Christian priest is able to introduce! (*Aside, only to Paranasius*): Of course he wasn't.

PARANASIUS (*very confused*): Who?

ZAID (*in an explanatory tone*): In the first place, Jesus, the son of Mary, was never crucified on any cross.

PARANASIUS (*unable to believe what he is hearing*): Jesus Christ was not crucified?!

ZAID (*the same explanatory tone*): In the second place, Jesus was never killed.

PARANASIUS (*not understanding anything*): He was not killed?!

ZAID: How could he have been, when Allah lifted him up to heaven and allowed him to go on serving him?

PARANASIUS (*in amazement speaks without realising what he is saying*): Jesus Christ serves Allah?

ZAID: Many people say many things about him… But all admit that he was a very fervent Muslim.

WALDO (*the stopwatch. Referring to the minute allocated to Zaid's answer*): Expired.

PARANASIUS (*because of the shock provoked by Zaid's claims, he is capable only of emitting a groan and pressing his right hand to his heart*): Ooh-ah!

PICA: And so who was… Who was it who…

RAPHAEL (*"translates" what Pica means to say*): …invented…

PICA: …Christianity? …Mohammed?

MARCEL: He warned you from the start that he was a Muslim.

KIRILL (*with VOICE NUMBER 2, mimicking curiosity*): And so who was crucified in the place of Jesus?

CAIUS (*referring to Zaid*): Wouldn't it be a good thing to let him have a few more shots at the goal, during half-time?

(*They all look at Waldo, to find out whether he will allow Zaid to answer questions from the audience.*

In order to give Paranasius time to recover, Waldo makes a gesture to signal that he has nothing against all these shots at the goal during half-time.)

THE PRINCE (*indulgently, to Zaid*): Answer them, Your Holiness.

ZAID: Christianity was invented neither by Jesus nor by Mohammed, but by the Christian priests who falsified the Gospels.

GEORGE (*sincerely amazed that they are discussing such unimportant matters*): So what?

ZAID (*transfixes George with a furious look, then continues speaking*): Of course, even Jesus (*may Allah bless his name!*) is nothing more than a humble and obedient slave of Allah.

THE PRINCE (*trying to hide his disillusionment with the humble social origins of Jesus*): Well, if he is a slave…

ZAID: Allah replaced Jesus with another man at the very moment in which his enemies were getting ready to kill him… So well did Allah disguise Jesus' replacement that even Mary and his disciples thought that those killers had crucified Jesus himself.

(*Almost all the listeners freeze in astonishment.*)

PICA: And who was crucified in Jesus' place?

ZAID (*confidently and patiently, as though he were imparting the truth to children*): Judas Iscariot.

WALDO (*abandoning his solemn comportment for a moment*): I have never heard anything so stupid in my entire life! …Why not Napoleon Bonaparte?

KIRILL (*with VOICE NUMBER 2, mockingly*): Bonaparte was a bit of a podgy fellow. His limbs would have been too short, spoiling all those mediaeval paintings.

(*The state of Paranasius' health has improved.*
    Waldo observes this and allows the Orthodox priest to return to the theological head to head.)

WALDO (*to the members of his group and to Zaid*): The break is over.
(*To Paranasius, with the sympathy that can sometimes be found among old acquaintances*): Time for your commentary, Lollipop of the Devils!

PARANASIUS (*to Waldo, with the same sort of sympathy, as though he were giving him a greeting*): The worms, father…

(*Waldo starts the stopwatch for Paranasius' minute of comments on Zaid's answer.*)

PARANASIUS (*with all the fury that has gathered in him. To Zaid and those in the ward*): Cursed be the Satans who would distort these holy truths! …Because of the ancestral sin of Adam, God grew wroth with the descendants of Adam and men began to die without hope of resurrection… Sent by God the Father, Our Saviour Jesus Christ was incarnated in a man. By His sacrifice on the Holy Cross, he took upon Himself all our sins. And he reconciled us with God, the Holy Trinity…

RAPHAEL (*thoughtfully*): Jesus Christ, is He also God?

PARANASIUS (*amiably*): Of course.

CAIUS (*sincerely, seeking to be helpful*): For them, they are all God. They're good blokes.

THE PRINCE (*to Paranasius*): What kind of God do you have, if you yourself claim that your God is dead?!

PARANASIUS (*jumps as though scalded*): He is not dead! …How could he be…

CAIUS (*interrupting Paranasius*): Didn't you say He was crucified?

PARANASIUS: Jesus Christ was killed, but God the Father resurrected Him! …

WALDO (*interrupting Paranasius. Looking at the stopwatch, he refers to the*

minute for commentary accorded to the Orthodox priest): Expired!
(*However many furious gestures Paranasius makes, he does not dare go against the interdiction imposed by Waldo, that of not uttering a single word more.*)

PICA (*taking up the last statement made by Paranasius. At first, he speaks unusually correctly and fluently, then he gets bogged down*): If He resurrected Him, God the Father is more pow... powerful than Jesus Christ! and i... i...

RAPHAEL (*clearly "translating" for Pica. He is merely saying the words that the stuttering Pica wishes to utter*): ...And if He is more powerful... (*following what Pica is struggling to enunciate. These words are addressed to Paranasius*) ... the Holy Trinity – about which you keep teaching us – is nothing but a... It is a... (*He hesitates, without knowing why.*)

ZOLI (*hastening to finish for him*): ...A wonder?

PARANASIUS: ...Supreme Being?

THE PRINCE: ...A mystery?

RAPHAEL (*continuing to "translate" what Pica clearly wishes to say*): ...No. A fraud!

(*Blinded by the fury that has gradually been building in him, Paranasius takes one step to the side, towards the spectators of the match and makes to rush at Pica. At the last moment, he thinks better of it and changes the direction of his attack at the very moment Raphael says that the Holy Trinity is a fraud. Paranasius attacks Raphael. He clasps his fingers around Raphael's throat and shakes him with the power of fury. Raphael resists, but with meagre results.*
    Merely in order not to delay the finale of the theological battle pointlessly, Kirill, Caius and George condescend to remove themselves to the site of the incident. They free Raphael from the hands of Paranasius. Then they take Paranasius back to his place in the middle of the ward, seating him face to face with Zaid.)

KIRILL (*with VOICE NUMBER 2, to Paranasius*): Leave it. You'll kill him later. First you have to save him.

CAIUS (*slipping a last piece of advice to Zaid before the head to head*): Place it at eleven yards, and kick it as hard as you can. Right at the whites of his eyes!

MARCEL (*doing the same thing with Paranasius*): Get into goal and deflect it! (*Looking very carefully at Paranasius and then at Zaid*): 'Cause you're ugly. But he's twice as ugly as you.

WALDO (*has his arm raised. When he starts the stopwatch with his left hand, he lowers his right arm, giving the signal to Zaid that he can begin to formulate the last of the three questions he is entitled to*): Kick off!

ZAID (*weighing his words with great seriousness. Then he casts a circular look at the spectators*): I ask about what you also have observed… The pagans have many gods. They worship any trifle that catches their fancy. (*Addressing Paranasius*): How many gods do you have?

PARANASIUS: The sole true God… One alone!

ZAID (*with warmth in his voice*): Is it for you also a mistake to deal with someone who is not God as though he were God?!

PARANASIUS (*seeming to detect an improvement in the imam's comportment*): What did I teach you?! (*Convinced that Zaid is asking him about Allah.*) It is the most sickening depravation!

(*Continuing to monitor the stopwatch, Waldo indicates by a small sign that he is allowing Zaid and Paranasius to use up their minute for questions and their minute for answers in these successive short questions and answers.*)

ZAID (*with the same conciliatory attitude towards Paranasius*): Let's not mention Jesus… Tell me honestly: do you sometimes worship the Holy Spirit?

PARANASIUS (*defensive tone, seeking to give lessons to Zaid*): Do not the Holy Scriptures enjoin us to "pray ceaselessly"?

ZAID: Do you also pray ceaselessly to the one you call the Mother of God?

PARANASIUS (*modestly*): Ceaselessly, no. But very often. Day and night.

ZAID: To the Apostles, for example, to Peter and Paul, do you pray?

PARANASIUS (*half joking, half in earnest*): God forbid that Paul should hear that you pray only to Peter.

ZAID (*with the same almost servile attitude, of someone who begs instruction from one wiser than himself*): But to the saints? Why do you need to pray also to them?

PARANASIUS: Well, all day long, the saints converse with God, just as I am with you. All it would take would be for one of them to say: "What a pig-dog that Zaid has become!" and straightaway you would find yourself in the jaws of hell (*With a more colloquial language, in order to win Zaid's esteem.*) In any case, prayers to them are not much use unless you kiss the relics of the saints a little.

ZAID (*becoming enraged. He barely manages to conceal his revulsion*): What?! To kiss the bones of the dead?

PARANASIUS (*not noticing Zaid's agitation*): Some have more flesh on them than you do.

PICA: They have too much… they should make us each a stew.

PARANASIUS (*bores Pica with wrathful eyes, then resumes in the encouraging tone with which he has been offering advice to Zaid*): Whoever bows to the fragrant, undecaying holy relics, receives blessings, health and all the bounties of the Holy Trinity.

(*Suddenly, Waldo silently points: the two minutes, the first belonging to Zaid, for the question, and the second belonging to Paranasius, for the answer, have come to an end.*

Waldo then jabs his finger in the direction of Zaid, indicating to him that he has begun to time the minute Zaid has to comment on the answer given by Paranasius.)

ZAID (*changing the sweet tone he has been using in order to worm secrets out of Paranasius into a tone of the blackest condemnation, he addresses Paranasius*): If a man robs his benefactor…

(*From now on, Paranasius adopts a peculiar attitude.*
He barricades himself against his enemy's attack, swivelling round so that his side is towards Zaid. He puts his finger in his left ear. With his right hand, he shakes his cross, as though against the devil. And he begins to repeat a word in order to drown out the enemy's intervention.)

PARANASIUS (*in salvoes of two and then three*): Liar-liar! Liar-liar-liar!

ZAID (*for a moment astonished, but not allowing himself to deviate from his wrath*): If a man robs his benefactor, he is despised… He who betrays his country is annihilated… The pagans know they have many idols, but nevertheless, they compare them, in their darkened minds, with things of honour.

PARANASIUS (*as before*): Liar-liar! Liar-liar-liar! …Liar-liar! Liar-liar-liar! …

ZAID: …You, however, compare the Incomparable with the most disgusting carcasses… Exactly at the same time as you say: I don't have three, I don't have fifty-six… I have the sole and true God.

PARANASIUS (*in the same position as before*): That is true!

ZAID (*seething*): …Now listen to me: There will come a time when both your life. And your death. And even those who will smite you… Will be convulsed with loathing… Merely for having had anything to do with you!

(*Seeking to please their masters, i.e. Waldo and the other three individuals in the group of conspirators, Lupu and Zoli rush to attack and mock Paranasius and Zaid.)*

LUPU (*in derision. He speaks in imitation of Paranasius and addresses Zaid*): No one asked you to have anything to do with me. What are you doing coming into my Heaven?

ZOLI (*the same as Lupu. He speaks in imitation of Zaid and addresses Paranasius*): What are you doing in Paradise, O accursed?! ...I seek shelter with Allah against the whispers and cunning of that devil Paranasius!

CAIUS (*with a resounding voice, makes the following announcement to all present*): Ladies and gentlemen! Behold how the World War of Religions – as old as the history of mankind – has now come to an end before your very eyes! ...The assassinations have ceased, the wounds have healed, each of us is waiting with our suitcase at our feet to be lifted up to the Heavens! ...But before we can at last live in clover in Paradise, we must first traverse the barriers of devils above us. Whether the Muslim or whether the Orthodox will be the one to guide us to Heaven, helping us skirt this obstacle, there is only one way we can find out: Ladies and gentlemen, let us now hear Waldo's verdict!

WALDO (*very calm, seated at the table from where he continues to dominate the entire assembly*): Not yet... First put on their spectacles for the mind's eyes and take the holy finalists for a little walk!

(*Kirill brings from the tent inscribed "GOVERNMENT" two little canvas bags and a few pieces of string. The bags each have a hole that can be fitted over the nose when the bag has been pulled over the head. Each bag has a drawstring, which can pull tight the mouth of the bag, preventing the person whose head is inside from seeing any light.*

The conspirators put a bag over Zaid's head.)

GEORGE (*mockingly, to Zaid*): Bend over, Your Numbskull Enlightenment, so that we can fit your underpants over his head.

(*The proud Zaid says nothing and does not even resist very hard.*
Worried, Paranasius looks all around him, but seeing that he has nowhere to run, he remains where he is, dignified.)

KIRILL (*with VOICE NUMBER 2, to his colleagues, who surround Zaid*):
Attach the wing supports. So that his arms won't bother him when flying.

(*George and Caius tie Zaid's hands behind his back, and get ready to immobilise Paranasius.*)

PARANASIUS (*looking at the bag which George and Caius are ready to put over his head*): We Orthodox are accustomed to assisting the worldly powers, so give it to me and I'll tie it myself.

(*No sooner said than done. Paranasius is allowed to place the bag over his own head. Then the commando of conspirators gently tighten the drawstring of the bag around his throat. They adjust the orifice so that he will be able to breathe, and tie his hands behind his back.*)

KIRILL (*shouts at Paranasius and Zaid, around whom a small convoy has formed, ready to walk them as Waldo has commanded*): Bid farewell, fathers, to this world, but, after that, return to the aerodrome.

(*In the convoy, the people are arranged in the following order: at its head is Caius; in his right hand he holds two lengths of string, to which are tied Paranasius and Zaid, who advance behind him shuffling their feet, because their heads are hooded and their hands tied behind their backs.*

Behind Paranasius and Zaid, in their leash and with the same canine behaviour, advance Lupu and Zoli. George brings up the rear, holding the leash. Lupu and Zoli bark at Paranasius and Zaid. With their lips, George and then Caius imitate a brass band playing a march.

Those in the unaligned group draw closer, even standing, for a few moments, to the right and left of the convoy.

Passing the tents and then the beds, the convoy with Caius at its head and George at its rear makes a circuit of the entire ward.

While the convoy is parading, Kirill, standing by the table, converses with Waldo in a whisper.

At the moment when the convoy finishes its circuit of the ward, George and Caius leave Paranasius and Zaid back where they started, at a respectful distance, and approach the table, joining the whispered discussion between Kirill and Waldo.)

In their guise as dogs, Lupu and Zoli fulfil the task of guarding Paranasius and Zaid.

After the conspiratorial discussion between Waldo, Kirill, George and Caius concludes, the four raise their heads and look over at Paranasius and Zaid.)

KIRILL (speaking to those in his group regarding Paranasius and Zaid): What's the latest with the Saviours?

GEORGE (pulls his handkerchief only halfway out of his mouth, so that what he answers is unclear, but it is clear that it is something vulgar): They're…

CAIUS (understanding what is expected of him, joins the game): They've started their engines.

KIRILL: That means they can hardly wait to transport us to Paradise. *(Kirill looks at Waldo, to check whether he approves of what he is about to say. As Waldo – from a huge feeling of superiority – neither approves nor disapproves, it means that in fact he approves. Kirill addresses George and Caius regarding Paranasius and Zaid)*: Bring them a bit closer, and don't let them take off without the cargo.

(Kirill, George and Caius, accompanied by Lupu and Zoli, lead Paranasius and Zaid to the place where they had confronted each other theologically a short time before. Paranasius and Zaid are made to sit shoulder to shoulder, with their faces, although still covered, towards the table at which Waldo is enthroned.

The crowbars reappear. Kirill fetches them from the tent inscribed "GOVERNMENT" and distributes them to each member of the group of conspirators. Using – but gently – the iron bars, the edges of their palms, and the sides of their feet, Kirill, George and Caius hit Paranasius and Zaid on the back of the knees to make them kneel. They press down on their shoulders, and prop them up in a stable position when they slide to the left or right.

Those in the unaligned group – Marcel, the Prince, Pica and Raphael – come closer to see what will happen to Paranasius and Zaid, and form a semicircle around them.)

CAIUS (adopting Kirill's manner of speaking as he takes part in making Paranasius and Zaid kneel): Kneel down, Saviours, so that you can have a longer runway to gather speed.

(Waldo and the other conspirators will conduct themselves in such a way as to make Zaid and Paranasius believe that they are taking off and soaring vertically at great speed towards Paradise.)

WALDO (with a commanding tone): Start!

GEORGE (referring to Zaid and Paranasius): Look! They're off, like from the barrel of a gun.

KIRILL (always with VOICE NUMBER 2, where not explicitly stated that he is speaking with VOICE NUMBER 1): Let's keep close. Hold each other's hands so that we won't be scattered in the upper atmosphere.

PICA (speaking to Marcel, the Prince and Raphael and referring to the group of conspirators): Just wait, if Olympia catches them!

MARCEL (to Pica): Come off it, what can she do to them?! Take them to hospital.

GEORGE (nudging Zaid): Feel anything?

ZAID (his voice can be heard under the canvas bag): …No.

KIRILL (about Zaid): He's a modest lad. He doesn't want to be praised for flying more elegantly than Mohammed.

CAIUS (to Zaid and Paranasius): Lean your heads to the right or left, because we're arriving at the passes of Heaven.

GEORGE (thrusting Paranasius and Zaid in the direction he shouts): Right!

CAIUS (likewise): Left!

KIRILL (the same): Veer right!

GEORGE *(in the same way)*: Veer right again!

WALDO (to Zaid and Paranasius): Between us and Paradise there are Three Heavens. Soon you will feel the outer part of the floors of the First Heaven. Inform me who touches it first.

PARANASIUS (to Waldo): I think I passed mine twenty minutes ago…

KIRILL (to Paranasius): Any blood? (He checks the cloth of the bag, feeling it inside and out.) If you had already hit it…

GEORGE (continuing Kirill's line): …It would be gushing more than a barrel… (Hearing the word "barrel", he salivates and cannot continue.)

KIRILL (speaking in the manner of George, finishes the line): …And you'd snuff it, fuck it.

CAIUS (at his shout, the group of conspirators nip Zaid and Paranasius, as though they were being pecked by birds of prey): Flock of eagles!

ZAID (trying to fend them off with his hands and words): Eagles do not fly in flocks.

GEORGE: These ones mustn't have read the Koran.

KIRILL (shouts a warning to Zaid and Paranasius): Shower of meteorites!

(The conspirators poke Zaid and Paranasius in the sides with the tips of their iron bars and punch them. Waldo makes a curt gesture to calm the attack. Silence descends.)

KIRILL (shouts as though he were a lumberjack announcing a falling tree): Co-o-o-o-mi-i-i-i-ing!

CAIUS (shouts as though he were announcing the detonation of a charge of dynamite): Bu-u-u-urn-i-i-i-i-ing!

(Then an even greater silence. Insupportable tension.)

ZAID (although nothing unusual has happened, announces as though he had reached the First Heaven): Me!

PARANASIUS (not to be left out): No, me!

ZAID (in order to convince them that he has reached the First Heaven): I descry the arbours of Paradise, watered by rivers of water beneath and rivers of wine and honey above… Here the Muslims are coupling with comely virgins and the angels are flying around the Throne, crying: "Glory to Allah, Lord of the Ages!"

(Waldo gives a signal, ordering Kirill and George to hit Zaid and Paranasius over the head with their iron bars, both at the same time. Kirill and George each deliver a light blow to the tops of Zaid's and Paranasius' heads.

The victims fall: Zaid on all fours, Paranasius sideways, to the left. After leaving them for a few seconds to sprawl, they lift Zaid and Paranasius up and support them so that they can kneel once more.)

WALDO (calm announcement): That was the First Heaven.

KIRILL (about Zaid and Paranasius, in order to maintain the illusion that they are rising to Paradise): …They have recommenced their ascent!

PARANASIUS (referring to the Second Heaven): I have reached it!

ZAID: I've reached it too!

PARANASIUS (grandiosely and with visionary spirit): I see hosts of people glorifying God in the Garden of Heaven… With candles in their hands and tears of joy in their eyes. And. If I look more closely, I see they are Orthodox priests.

MARCEL: Ha!

PICA: Aren't they glorifying with communion bread?

THE PRINCE: Why Orthodox priests?

PARANASIUS: Because to serve as an Orthodox priest is higher than the service of the angels in Heaven. Because not even the angels can celebrate the Holy Liturgy and administer the Holy Sacraments, as the priests and bishops do, assisted by the deacons.

GEORGE: Is that right?

KIRILL: Angel, Paranasius is approaching!

CAIUS (*shouts as though he were announcing an incoming shell*): Whi-i-i-i-iz-i-i-ing!

(*A moment of silence. Unbearable tension.*

Then Kirill and Caius let their iron bars fall, with not much force, first on the head of Paranasius then on the head of Zaid. Zaid and Paranasius crash to the floor senseless.)

WALDO: That was the Second Heaven.

MARCEL (*to those in his group, the unaligned*): Let's redistribute the beds, after they move this lot to prison.

PICA (*likewise, speaking to the group of the unaligned and referring to the group of conspirators*): Or they make them gnaw the grass in a cemetery.

WALDO (*in the direction of Zaid and Paranasius*): But you have not yet reached the true Heaven. Because, as a rule, you get there after you die. (*Zaid and Paranasius are once more hauled up groaning onto their knees.*)

CAIUS (*referring in his old way to Zaid and Paranasius, to suggest that they are resuming their flight towards the Third Heaven*): Shall I refuel them?

KIRILL: Refuel them? First we'll have to catch up with them.

GEORGE: At this speed, their clothes are burning up like matchsticks. (*Moment of silence. Once more, unbearable tension.*

This time, as though in mockery, Kirill and George hit Zaid and Paranasius over the head with their iron bars so gently that they barely touch them.)

WALDO (*with barely noticeable irony*): The Third Heaven is always gentler.

CAIUS: Ladies and gentlemen! Please disembark: …Heaven!

KIRILL (*to Zaid*): You are at the very foot of Allah's throne. What is your greatest wish?

ZAID: Alas! …Might I hear the voice of Allah, blessed be his name?

CAIUS (*speaking as though he were Allah*): Yes, Zaid. Everything I passed down to you, you learned inside out. It's as if I'd been a barkeeper, and you'd taught people not to drink alcohol.

GEORGE (*frozen in amazement*): That's exactly what he taught us. (To Zaid, referring to Caius as though he really were Allah): See, what a decent bloke your God is? …

KIRILL (*to Zaid, continuing George's line*): And you deceived his trust…

GEORGE (*sincere in what he says about Zaid*): He's mad.

WALDO: If he's mad, take him to one side. I'll deal with him later.

PARANASIUS (*hearing his voice, he addresses Waldo*): And have I brought you, my son, into Heaven?

KIRILL (*answering Paranasius in Waldo's place*): Yes, it's quite nifty up here. Lots of floozies, who've climbed up into my lap, they're old slappers, like Zaid's hags.

PARANASIUS (*askance, to Kirill*): You're a bit of a devil. I don't know how they could have left the Gates ajar. But you say you're a friend of St Peter…

CAIUS (*his voice vibrating with importance, to the Orthodox priest*): Paranasius, you are in front of your threefold bundle gods...

KIRILL (*in the same manner, to Paranasius*): ...But the Holy Spirit has popped out to Christianise some Catholics and he asks you to excuse him...

CAIUS (*the same, to Paranasius*): ...Ask God your most ardent wish.

PARANASIUS: Before the Almighty? ...Almighty God. After I have been declared a saint, make the icons with my image not heal the good. But rather strike down the wicked... Let them break the arm of one. Let them burst the eyes of another. And let them make the head of a certain man I know, with a handkerchief in his mouth, fall off.

GEORGE (*to the Orthodox priest, realising that he is referring to him*): Is that any way to talk in Heaven? (*To those in his group*): He's mad.

KIRILL: No problem. If he's mad, Waldo will deal with him.

CAIUS (*making an announcement*): Ladies and gentlemen! This is how it is with people: you know that each and every one of us feels as though, every ten minutes, he has been carried off by a band of demons. Beaten until he vomits blood. Brought back unawares. And nevertheless, no one has the courage to talk about this feeling. Behold wherein resides the success of religion! ...

KIRILL: ...Ladies and gentlemen! These two men (*points at Zaid and Paranasius*) presented themselves here and swore that they, together with their religions, would rid us of our flocks of demons...

CAIUS (*continues the announcement, reproducing an imaginary dialogue*): "How quickly?" "Very quickly. In the blink of an eye." "Really?" "Well, isn't it taught that as soon as they see us we start casting the profound truths of our religions at them and in three or four minutes there won't be a single devil left in the world..."

GEORGE (*sensing it is his turn to improvise something, takes a deep breath, but only manages to say*): …Yes.

KIRILL: …Praise to you Paranasius and your gods! Praise to you Zaid and your God! For you are so skilled at hanging the skins of all the devils from a single stick! … And we let them do their stuff… Each of them for three or four minutes once. Each of them for three or four minutes twice. They had time to do their stuff a hundred times more than they requested… And now, at the end of the Festival of Meetings, what do we ascertain? …

CAIUS: …Not only that the devils that have been tormenting everyone have not vanished. But that they brought from home, from their religions, even greater herds of devils! …

KIRILL: …If you look hard enough, behind every object that exists on Earth, there are devils…

MARCEL: You said it with your own mouth. Behind every medical expert in particular there is an endless column of devils.

KIRILL: Marcel, for example, is all wrapped up in devils, like a woman dressed up in a fur coat…

PICA (*leaping to the aid of Marcel, addresses Kirill*): What are you saying? Maybe it's your shadow that falls on his face.

CAIUS: …We're covered in illness, suffering, death and devils, like an abandoned table covered with dust…

KIRILL: …On Earth, the devils swarm everywhere…

CAIUS: …The religions not only do not destroy the devils, but, behind the scenes, the religions and the devils passionately kiss…

GEORGE: …They stick their lowborn tongues in each other's ears…

CAIUS: …And three quarters of the world's most dangerous devils are goaded against people precisely by religions! …

THE PRINCE (*with interest, to Zaid and Paranasius*): Is that what you do?

RAPHAEL: Not all religions…

(*The gazes of all the patients continue to be directed at Waldo. He allows two or three moments to pass in order to increase the effect of his intervention.*)

WALDO (*shrugs, as though he were saying that, although the verdict he is passing might seem cruel, there is no way he can avoid it*): Surgical treatment!

(*Standing behind their victims, Kirill and George raise their iron bars and deal a mortal blow to the heads of Zaid and Paranasius. Caius also strikes. Waldo rises from the table. He is holding an iron bar. He approaches the two fallen bodies. He applies the coup-de-grace first to the skull of Paranasius, second to the skull of Zaid.*

In the ward, the lights begin to dim. The Festival of Meetings has come to a close. The two corpses remain in the middle of the stage. George, Kirill and Caius tidy up a little, and withdraw to the tents. George, Kirill and Caius enter the tent inscribed "GOVERNMENT". Waldo vanishes into the tent inscribed "HEAVEN". Rattling their chains, Lupu and Zoli take shelter under the beds by the tents. Marcel, Pica, the Prince and Raphael also withdraw, each climbing into his own bed. They stretch out, and wrap themselves in their covers, seeking the most comfortable position. Their voices become sleepy.)

THE PRINCE: And so who won in the end?

PICA: I had a friend who was r-r-read to me from a b-b-book.

RAPHAEL (*repeats and corrects the words uttered by Pica*): I had a friend who read to me from a book…

PICA: That, with all the f-f-fury-ness that is Earth…

RAPHAEL (*as before*): That, against all the fury that is on Earth…

PICA: Je-Jehova God says to man: …

RAPHAEL (*in the same manner*): Jehovah God says to man: …

PICA: "Be not afraid. And d-d-don't fear. Be strong… And take heart."

RAPHAEL (*as before*): "Be not afraid. And do not fear. Be strong. And take heart."

PICA: "Behold. Soon I come."

RAPHAEL (*in the same way*): "Behold. Soon I come."

CURTAIN

The Author

Daniel Bănulescu (born 1960). He has published three volumes of poetry: *Te voi iubi pînă la sfîrşitul patului (I shall Love you until the End of the Bed)* (1993), *Balada lui Daniel Bănulescu (The Ballad of Daniel Bănulescu)* (1997), *Republica Federală Daniel Bănulescu. Statul de Nord & Statul de Sud (The Federal Republic of Daniel Bănulescu. The Northern State and the Southern State)* (2000), *Daniel, al rugăciunii (Daniel, of the Prayer)* (2002); and the novels: *Te pup în fund, Conducător iubit! (I Kiss your Arse, Beloved Leader!)* (1994) and *Cei şapte regi ai orasului Bucureşti (The Seven Kings of the City of Bucharest)* (1997).

A member of the Romanian Writers' Union, he has been awarded the Romanian Academy Prize for Literature. Together with Ernest Wichner, he was awarded the City of Munster European Poetry Prize in 2005. A collection of his poetry has been translated and published in German: *Schrumpeln wirst du wirst eine exatische Frucht sein* (Pro Procura, Vienna, 2002 and 2005), and also the novel *Ich Küsser dir den Hintern, Geliebter Führer!*

The Translator

Alistair Ian Blyth was born in Sunderland in 1970 and educated at Bede School, Cambridge University (BA), and Durham University (MA). From Romanian he has translated a number of works, including *An Intellectual History of Cannibalism* by Cătălin Avramescu (Princeton University Press), the novel *Little Fingers* by Filip Florian (Houghton-Mifflin Harcourt), the novel *Our Circus Presents...* by Lucian Dan Teodorovici (Dalkey Archive Press), *Aunt Varvara's Clients: Clandestine Histories* by Stelian Tănase (Spuyten Duyvil), and two books by Constantin Noica; *Six Maladies of the Contemporay Spirit* (University of Plymouth Press) and *The Becoming within Being* (Marquette UP). His most recent translation is Filip and Matei Florian's *Băiuţ Alley Lads* (University of Plymouth Press). He lives in Bucharest.

Hardback edition first published in the United Kingdom in 2010 by University of Plymouth Press, Scott Building, Drake Circus, Plymouth, Devon, PL4 8AA, United Kingdom.

ISBN 978-1-84102-212-3

Series Editor: Anthony Caleshu
Translation: Alistair Ian Blyth
Publisher: Paul Honeywill
Publishing Assistant: Victoria Halliday
Series Art Director: Sarah Chapman
Consulting Editor: Liz Wells

Typeset by University of Plymouth in Janson 10/14pt
Printed and bound by R. Booth Limited, Penryn, Cornwall

Visit www.uppress.co.uk/romanian.htm to learn more about this series

Published with the support of the Romanian Cultural Institute

20 Romanian Writers
2009 - 2013

Publications November 2009

Occurrence in the Immediate Unreality
Max Blecher

ISBN 978-1-84102-207-9 Hardback

This autobiographical fiction offers an intimate and unsettling account of Blecher's ideas of self-identity and the body. He explores the 'crisis of unreality' in relation to the human condition and shares his adolescent experiences of physical infirmity, social isolation and sexual awakening.

Six Maladies of the Contemporary Spirit
Constantin Noica

Posthumously awarded the Herder Prize, 1988
ISBN 978-1-84102-203-1 Hardback

In this unique work, Noica analyses history, culture and the individual in what he describes as the fundamental precariousness of being. 'Maladies' of the spirit are no longer debilitating, but creative for our European interest in change, unity, and diversity.

The Cinematography Caravan
Ioan Groşan

Romanian Writers' Union, Prize for Prose, 1992
ISBN 978-1-84102-205-5 Hardback

A black comedy set in 1960s Romania: a Stalinist propaganda film truck rumbles into a forgotten village in Transylvania. The occupants of the village believe in the traditional values of church and God and are in no mood to participate, placing obstacles in the way of the Cinematography Caravan. However they soon realise the best way to deal with the representative of the communist party and these films is to cooperate.

Lines Poems Poetry
Mircea Ivănescu

Botoşani Mihai Eminescu National Poetry Prize, 1999
ISBN 978-1-84102-217-8 Hardback

Ivănescu's poetry represents the achievement of a little known master. Centring on a wide cast of characters including his alter ego 'mopete', Ivănescu's idiosyncratic, lyrical sensibility offers allusive, comic and elegiac meditations on our common lot.

November 2010

No Way Out of Hadesburg and other Poems
Ioan Es. Pop

Romanian Order of Cultural Merit, 2004
ISBN 978-1-84102-209-3 Hardback

Originally a teacher in a village called Hadesburg, Ioan Es. Pop expresses in his poetry his response to existence in Romania under communist control, forbidden to write but able to work as a builder on Ceauşescu's palace and living alone in a bachelor block. Pop's poetry is an autobiographical account of such a time, a life with no way out. The world of the poems is a closed, boundless imaginary space, charged with dramatic intensity and tempered by a bittersweet, compassionate existential angst.

Who Won the World War of Religions?
Daniel Bănulescu

City of Munster European Poetry Prize, 2005
ISBN 978-1-84102-212-3 Hardback

Contemporary madness in its entirety is summarised in Daniel Bănulescu's play, set in an asylum populated with twelve dangerous madmen who are divided as believers of the four major religions. This is theatre in a world governed by insanity; as Dan Stanca remarks, the play could be set anywhere - in Piteşti, in the Siberian Gulag, in a Nazi concentration camp, Maoist or Khmer Rouge extermination camp, and, even, in one of the CIA's secret prisons? This is the principal merit and black humour of the play.

The Băiut Alley Lads
Filip and Matei Florian

România Literară and Anonimul Foundation Prize for Debut Novel,
2004
ISBN 978-1-84102-219-2 Hardback

Following his prize-winning debut novel, Florian leaves the Romanian
village life behind and takes us to Băiut Alley in Bucharest.

Two brothers, Filip and Matei, are growing up in a totalitarian society.
Every day life is recounted through their young eyes. Their story is one
of childish naïvety set against a backdrop of life imposed by communism.
Their world is filled with characters from children's television, broadcast
by the official communist media, alongside magazines and cinema. 'Joe
Lemonade', 'Giani Morandi', 'Rome Specs' and 'Brooslee' accentuate
the absurdity and grotesqueness of their surroundings.

The brothers become close through a shared love of football,
supporting the same team, Dinamo Bucureşti. Ultimately, *The Băiut
Alley Lads* is a novel about miracles that take place within a nightmare,
regardless of whether they occur in an obscure lane in an obscure district
of a country kept in obscurity by communist dictatorship.

Auntie Varvara's Clients
Stelian Tănase

Awarded a Fulbright Scholarship, 1997
ISBN 978-1-84102-221-5 Hardback

The pre-communist nickname for the Siguranţă (Romanian Security
Service) was "Auntie Varvara", and so communist underground members
are literally "Auntie Varvara's clients" of the title.

Stelian Tănase explores Romania's communist 'roots of disaster'
from early illegal membership of the communist underground to their
eventual rise to power and the struggle for supremacy. Tănase sketches
a pattern of warring factions through an incredible swarm of characters
who abruptly fall completely silent after the final victory of Gheorghiu-
Dej and the formation of the communist police state and its hierarchy. A
Romania then on course for human disaster.

November 2011

Dazzler
Mircea Cărtărescu

Grand Officer of the Cultural Merit Order, awarded by the Romanian Presidency, 2006
ISBN 978-1-84102-206-2 Hardback

The first book in the Dazzler Trilogy describes a communist Bucharest awash with thrills and nightmares. Dazzler opens with a sixties bedroom view obscured by towering prefab blocks - a Romania in rupture. His writing is influenced by childhood memories; hearing the screams of political prisoners being interrogated and only now revisiting these places as they are gradually torn down. The essence of Cărtărescu is to capture the socialist capital leading up to the moment of its downfall.

Wasted Morning
Gabriela Adamesteanu

Romanian Writers' Union Prize for the Novel, 1983
ISBN 978-1-84102-211-6 Hardback

Wasted Morning is a truly modern novel, beginning and ending in the present yet resurrecting a Romania of the past. The story centres on Madam Vica Delcă who visits Ivona Scarlat. During this visit Ivona receives news of her husband's sudden death, triggering memories of the past which are then re-lived. Adamesteanu creates a world of old upper bourgeois Romania at the brink of World War One.

Small Changes in Attitude
Răzvan Petrescu

Grand Prize at the 1st Edition of the Camil Petrescu National Dramaturgic Competition; Romanian Writers' Union Prize for Theatre, 1995
ISBN 978-1-84102-214-7 Hardback

Răzvan Petrescu is cited by Adriana Bittel as one of Romania's finest short prose writers. This anthology of short fiction paints each story as a photographic reality and journeys from realistic black humor to the ironic and fantastic. This collection includes his 1989 debut, *Summer Garden, Eclipse*, a modern take on the biblical story of Cain and Abel, and 'Friday Afternoon' wherein an epidemic kills everyone in an apartment block. The title truly summarizes this anthology; Petrescu suggests small changes in attitude.

Anthology of Poems
Ion Mureşan

Romanian Writers' Union Prize for Poetry, 1993
ISBN 978-1-84102-213-0 Hardback

There is both an enigmatic and an original character to the poetic language of Ion Mureşan who concerns himself with the political nature of Romanian poetry in this anthology. Mureşan's poetry draws upon Transylvanian legends to address the communist manipulation and monopoly of truth by regaining individual thought through his poetry, which reflects upon what it is to be Romanian.

November 2012

Silent Escape and Impossible Escape
Lena Constante

Romanian Academy, Lucain Blaga Prize, 1993
ISBN 978-1-84102-216-1 Hardback

Lena Constante is one of the few women political prisoners to have written about her years of imprisonment. She describes in detail her physical and psychological humiliation and suffering in the solitary confinement common in communist Romania. The whole premise of this novel rests on Constante's ability to survive, to escape into her mind and on solidarity with other female inmates. A work of human survival against the odds.

French Themes
Nicolae Manolescu

Romanian Ambassador for UNESCO, 2006
Romanian Academy Member, 2007
ISBN 978-1-84102-208-6 Hardback

Inspired by the combination of political intrigue and love contained within the belles lettres of the great French novelists, Manolescu uses this recipe to tell the story of a great love. Cristina Cheveresan considers *French Themes* as "love declared or merely suggested, patient and durable, arousing the aromas of French perfumes but also a reading in culture and civilization".

The Iceberg of Modern Poetry
Gheorghe Crăciun

ASPRO Prize for the Year's Best Book of Criticism 1997, 2002
ISBN 978-1-84102-204-8 Hardback

Gheorghe Crăciun redefines modernist poetry through the analysis of Wordsworth and Coleridge, Baudelaire and Whitman. Through this Crăciun proposes a new direction for modern poetry, one that is in permanent tension. This eventually leads Crăciun to consider a third direction, one that revisits old traditions that are still reflected and reinflected in modern poetry. *The Iceberg of Modern Poetry* is a 500 page authoritative contribution to international debate on this subject.

Picturesque and Melancholy
Andrei Pleşu

Ordre national de la Légion d'Honneur, to the rank of Commandeur, and then Grand Officier, 1999
ISBN 978-1-84102-218-5 Hardback

Pleşu questions European culture through the aesthetic of melancholy and literary picturesque myths of Western culture. A controversial text at the time it was written, he approaches the topic from a philosophical stance with an exuberant writing style and an undertow of the subversive. He fell out of favour with the communist regime and was banned from publishing which resulted in his exile to Tescani a community in Bacau, Moldova, Romania.

November 2013

Diary of Happiness
Nicolae Steinhardt

ISBN 978-1-84102-210-9 Hardback

Romania was not the place for a Jewish intellectual at a time when the regime was re-Stalinising. Steinhardt could have escaped prison if he became a witness for the prosecution in a communist show trial. He refused and was imprisoned in 1959 for 'high treason' and 'machinating against the socialist order'. These pages are an introspective diary of Steinhardt's prison years, as Romanian literary critic Mircea Martin explains, *Diary of Happiness* is not only a revelation of faith, but is also a revelation of freedom and of inner freedom.

Simion the Liftite
Petru Cimpoeşu

Romanian Writers' Union Prize of Cuvîntul, 2001
ISBN 978-1-84102-215-4 Hardback

This novel captures hope and despair in post-revolution Romania. Christ descends for three days at the height of the revolution in December 1989 and stands in the presidential election, offering himself as saviour and sacrifice once again. Mircea Iorgulescu says of Petru Cimpoeşu that there is a permanent ambiguity in this narrative, which never descends into caricature, but rather is viewed with understanding and even, quite often, warmth. The lack of aggression comes from aesthetic style. The serenity of tone here has its origin in the pure pleasure of constructing a story.

This title within the 20 Romanian Writers series is subject to change with another publication.

The Children's Crusade
Florina Ilis

România Literară and Anonimul Foundation Prize for Book of the Year, 2005
ISBN 978-1-84102-220-8 Hardback

A train is hijacked by children, who organise resistance against the authorities sent from Bucharest. In their attempts to negotiate, the authorities prove hypocritical, lacking any understanding of the children's demands. The novel presents a clash of ideologies relating to what it is to be Romanian and to the realities of life under Ceauşescu's communist rule. Ilis weaves two differing viewpoints together, reversing perspectives and constructing a world adrift.

Cioran Naïve and Sentimental
Ion Vartic

Romanian Writers' Union Prize, Cluj branch award, essay, 2004
ISBN 978-1-84102-222-2 Hardback

A biography of Emil Cioran, a philosopher and freethinker, born in Transylvania, who had an inferiority complex and was ashamed of his birthplace. Cioran was attracted to Western culture, because his perception was that Eastern European countries have always been dominated by Western European history. Vartic suggests that Cioran represents one extreme and that Romanians are proud of their cultural heritage, taking the virtues of home and making it theirs.